PARIS
TALKS

PARIS
TALKS

Addresses
Given by
'Abdu'l-Bahá
in 1911

Bahá'í
PUBLISHING

Wilmette, Illinois

Bahá'í Publishing
401 Greenleaf Ave, Wilmette, Illinois 60091
Copyright © 2006 by the National Spiritual Assembly
of the Bahá'ís of the United States
All rights reserved. Published 2006
Printed in the United States of America ∞
17   16   15   14   2   3   4

Library of Congress Cataloging-in-Publication Data

'Abdu'l-Bahá, 1844–1921.
    Paris talks : addresses given by 'Abdu'l-Bahá in 1911.
       p. cm.
    Includes index.
    ISBN-13: 978-1-931847-32-2 (alk. paper)
    ISBN-10: 1-931847-32-0 (alk. paper)
    1. Bahai Faith. I. Title.

BP363.A3 2006
297.9'3824—dc22

                               2006047703

Cover design by Pepper Oldziey
Book design by Patrick Falso

Contents

Part II

Part III

Introduction

Paris in 1911 was a city at the heart of a fast-changing continent. Europe in the early twentieth century was a place characterized by political instability and the convergence of numerous new ideologies that would shape the modern world as we know it. The rise of revolutionary political, social, artistic, and spiritual movements bore testament to a growing need among individuals to make sense of the world in which they lived.

In this setting, just a few years before the outbreak of the First World War, 'Abdu'l-Bahá—the son of Bahá'u'lláh, the Prophet and Founder of the Bahá'í Faith—made the series of extraordinary public addresses that are documented in this book. A prisoner since the age of nine, 'Abdu'l-Bahá had shared a lifetime of imprisonment and exile with his father at the hands of the Ottoman Empire. Two years after finally being freed from prison at the age of sixty-seven, unhindered by the poor health that was the result of a lifetime of hardship and suffering, he set out from Palestine (present-day Israel) on a momentous series of journeys to Europe and the United States. His purpose was to share the teachings and vision of Bahá'u'lláh with the people of the West.

At the time of 'Abdu'l-Bahá's visit to Paris, the Bahá'í Faith was a little-known, obscure religion of the East. Originating in Iran in the middle of the nineteenth century, it owes its origin to the labors of two successive founding Prophets: the Báb and Bahá'-u'lláh. As the former explained, His mission was to prepare the way for "Him Whom God shall make manifest," the Manifestation of God awaited by the followers of all faiths. During the course of successive waves of persecution that followed this announcement and that claimed the lives of the Báb and several thousands of His followers, Bahá'u'lláh declared Himself to be the fulfillment of the Divine promise.

In His Will and Testament, Bahá'u'lláh appointed 'Abdu'l-Bahá to succeed Him in leading the Bahá'í community and to be the interpreter of His writings. It was in this capacity that 'Abdu'l-Bahá journeyed to Europe and gave his audiences a glimpse of the new faith and its teachings. Spending nine weeks in Paris from October 3 until December 2, 1911, 'Abdu'l-Bahá addressed crowds of people from all walks of life in a manner that transcended cultural barriers. Speaking in Persian with the aid of a translator, he shared profound insights on a number of topics in a simple manner, accessible to anyone who listened with an open heart. 'Abdu'l-Bahá spoke on matters of spirituality as well as on the condition of the world. He shed light on complex matters of the soul and the spiritual nature of man, while addressing issues concerning society at large.

Among the topics covered in the talks are human nature, the soul, the Prophets of God, prophecies concerning the return of Christ, racial and religious prejudices, material and spiritual progress, pain and sorrow, the causes of war, and the duty of everyone to strive for peace. 'Abdu'l-Bahá gave his audiences a concise overview of the teachings of the Bahá'í Faith and discussed such principles as the independent investigation of the truth, the unity of mankind, the harmony of science and religion, the abolition of all forms of prejudice, the equality of the sexes, and universal peace.

The transcripts of the talks were compiled from notes taken by four British visitors—Lady Sarah Louisa Blomfield; her two daughters, Mary Esther and Rose Ellinor Cecilia; and Beatrice Marion Platt. The book was first published in 1912 at the suggestion of 'Abdu'l-Bahá and has since been translated into a number of languages. Though the collection originally included only the talks of 'Abdu'l-Bahá given in Paris (parts I and II), several talks and a tablet recorded during his subsequent visit to England (part III) have also come to be included over the years.

In the years since the talks were delivered, the Bahá'í Faith has emerged as a youthful and dynamic worldwide community with more than five million adherents. Today Bahá'ís reside in virtually every corner of the globe and are united in following and promoting the teachings of 'Abdu'l-Baha and his father. 'Abdu'l-Bahá's words—both spiritually uplifting and thought-provoking—are as poignant today as they were when he spoke them, and history continues to shed light on the truth of his striking admonitions. Long considered a classic within the Bahá'í community, *Paris Talks* is now being made widely available to a general audience for the first time so that it may offer assurance and inspiration to a new generation of readers and continue to shed light on some of the most perplexing issues facing society today.

PARIS
TALKS

PART I

1

THE DUTY OF KINDNESS AND SYMPATHY TOWARDS STRANGERS AND FOREIGNERS

October 16th and 17th, 1911

When a man turns his face to God he finds sunshine everywhere. All men are his brothers. Let not conventionality cause you to seem cold and unsympathetic when you meet strange people from other countries. Do not look at them as though you suspected them of being evildoers, thieves and boors. You think it necessary to be very careful, not to expose yourselves to the risk of making acquaintance with such, possibly, undesirable people.

I ask you not to think only of yourselves. Be kind to the strangers, whether come they from Turkey, Japan, Persia, Russia, China or any other country in the world.

Help to make them feel at home; find out where they are staying, ask if you may render them any service; try to make their lives a little happier.

In this way, even if, sometimes, what you at first suspected should be true, still go out of your way to be kind to them— this kindness will help them to become better.

5

5   After all, why should any foreign people be treated as strangers?

6   Let those who meet you know, without your proclaiming the fact, that you are indeed a Bahá'í.

7   Put into practice the Teaching of Bahá'u'lláh, that of kindness to all nations. Do not be content with showing friendship in words alone, let your heart burn with loving kindness for all who may cross your path.

8   Oh, you of the Western nations, be kind to those who come from the Eastern world to sojourn among you. Forget your conventionality when you speak with them; they are not accustomed to it. To Eastern peoples this demeanor seems cold, unfriendly. Rather let your manner be sympathetic. Let it be seen that you are filled with universal love. When you meet a Persian or any other stranger, speak to him as to a friend; if he seems to be lonely try to help him, give him of your willing service; if he be sad console him, if poor succor him, if oppressed rescue him, if in misery comfort him. In so doing you will manifest that not in words only, but in deed and in truth, you think of all men as your brothers.

9   What profit is there in agreeing that universal friendship is good, and talking of the solidarity of the human race as a grand ideal? Unless these thoughts are translated into the world of action, they are useless.

10   The wrong in the world continues to exist just because people talk only of their ideals, and do not strive to put them into practice. If actions took the place of words, the world's misery would very soon be changed into comfort.

11   A man who does great good, and talks not of it, is on the way to perfection.

The man who has accomplished a small good and magnifies it in his speech is worth very little. 12

If I love you, I need not continually speak of my love—you will know without any words. On the other hand if I love you not, that also will you know—and you would not believe me, were I to tell you in a thousand words, that I loved you. 13

People make much profession of goodness, multiplying fine words because they wish to be thought greater and better than their fellows, seeking fame in the eyes of the world. Those who do most good use fewest words concerning their actions. 14

The children of God do the works without boasting, obeying His laws. 15

My hope for you is that you will ever avoid tyranny and oppression; that you will work without ceasing till justice reigns in every land, that you will keep your hearts pure and your hands free from unrighteousness. 16

This is what the near approach to God requires from you, and this is what I expect of you. 17

2

THE POWER AND VALUE OF TRUE THOUGHT DEPEND UPON ITS MANIFESTATION IN ACTION

October 18th

The reality of man is his thought, not his material body. The   1
thought force and the animal force are partners. Although
man is part of the animal creation, he possesses a power of
thought superior to all other created beings.

If a man's thought is constantly aspiring towards heavenly   2
subjects then does he become saintly; if on the other hand his
thought does not soar, but is directed downwards to center
itself upon the things of this world, he grows more and more
material until he arrives at a state little better than that of a
mere animal.

Thoughts may be divided into two classes: 3
(1st) Thought that belongs to the world of thought alone.   4
(2nd) Thought that expresses itself in action.   5
Some men and women glory in their exalted thoughts, but   6
if these thoughts never reach the plane of action they remain
useless: the power of thought is dependent on its manifes-

tation in deeds. A philosopher's thought may, however, in the world of progress and evolution, translate itself into the actions of other people, even when they themselves are unable or unwilling to show forth their grand ideals in their own lives. To this class the majority of philosophers belong, their teachings being high above their actions. This is the difference between philosophers who are Spiritual Teachers, and those who are mere philosophers: the Spiritual Teacher is the first to follow His own teaching; He brings down into the world of action His spiritual conceptions and ideals. His Divine thoughts are made manifest to the world. His thought is Himself, from which He is inseparable. When we find a philosopher emphasizing the importance and grandeur of justice, and then encouraging a rapacious monarch in his oppression and tyranny, we quickly realize that he belongs to the first class: for he thinks heavenly thoughts and does not practice the corresponding heavenly virtues.

7   This state is impossible with Spiritual Philosophers, for they ever express their high and noble thoughts in actions.

3

GOD IS THE GREAT COMPASSIONATE PHYSICIAN WHO ALONE GIVES TRUE HEALING

October 19th

All true healing comes from God! There are two causes for sickness, one is material, the other spiritual. If the sickness is of the body, a material remedy is needed, if of the soul, a spiritual remedy. 1

If the heavenly benediction be upon us while we are being healed then only can we be made whole, for medicine is but the outward and visible means through which we obtain the heavenly healing. Unless the spirit be healed, the cure of the body is worth nothing. All is in the hands of God, and without Him there can be no health in us! 2

There have been many men who have died at last of the very disease of which they have made a special study. Aristotle, for instance, who made a special study of the digestion, died of a gastric malady. Avicenna was a specialist of the heart, but he died of heart disease. God is the great compassionate Physician who alone has the power to give true healing. 3

4   All creatures are dependent upon God, however great may seem their knowledge, power and independence.

5   Behold the mighty kings upon earth, for they have all the power in the world that man can give them, and yet when death calls they must obey, even as the peasants at their gates.

6   Look also at the animals, how helpless they are in their apparent strength! For the elephant, the largest of all animals, is troubled by the fly, and the lion cannot escape the irritation of the worm. Even man, the highest form of created beings, needs many things for his very life; first of all he needs air, and if he is deprived of it for a few minutes, he dies. He is also dependent on water, food, clothing, warmth, and many other things. On all sides he is surrounded by dangers and difficulties, against which his physical body alone cannot cope. If a man looks at the world around him, he will see how all created things are dependent and are captive to the laws of Nature.

7   Man alone, by his spiritual power, has been able to free himself, to soar above the world of matter and to make it his servant.

8   Without the help of God man is even as the beasts that perish, but God has bestowed such wonderful power upon him that he might ever look upward, and receive, among other gifts, healing from His divine Bounty.

9   But alas! man is not grateful for this supreme good, but sleeps the sleep of negligence, being careless of the great mercy which God has shown towards him, turning his face away from the light and going on his way in darkness.

10   It is my earnest prayer, that ye be not like unto this, but rather that ye keep your faces steadfastly turned to the light, so that ye may be as lighted torches in the dark places of life.

4

THE NEED FOR UNION
BETWEEN THE PEOPLES
OF THE EAST AND WEST

Friday, October 20th

'Abdu'l-Bahá said:

In the past, as in the present, the Spiritual Sun of Truth   1
has always shone from the horizon of the East.

Abraham appeared in the East. In the East Moses arose to   2
lead and teach the people. On the Eastern horizon arose the
Lord Christ. Muḥammad was sent to an Eastern nation. The
Báb arose in the Eastern land of Persia. Bahá'u'lláh lived and
taught in the East. All the great Spiritual Teachers arose in
the Eastern world. But although the Sun of Christ dawned
in the East the radiance thereof was apparent in the West,
where the effulgence of its glory was more clearly seen. The
divine light of His Teaching shone with a greater force in the
Western world, where it has made a more rapid headway than
in the land of its birth.

In these days the East is in need of material progress and the   3
West is in want of a spiritual idea. It would be well for the West

to turn to the East for illumination, and to give in exchange its scientific knowledge. There must be this interchange of gifts.

4   The East and the West must unite to give to each other what is lacking. This union will bring about a true civilization, where the spiritual is expressed and carried out in the material.

5   Receiving thus the one from the other the greatest harmony will prevail, all people will be united, a state of great perfection will be attained, there will be a firm cementing, and this world will become a shining mirror for the reflection of the attributes of God.

6   We all, the Eastern with the Western nations, must strive day and night with heart and soul to achieve this high ideal, to cement the unity between all the nations of the earth. Every heart will then be refreshed, all eyes will be opened, the most wonderful power will be given, the happiness of humanity will be assured.

7   We must pray that by the Bounty of God, Persia will be enabled to receive the material and mental civilization of the West, and by Divine Grace to give in return her spiritual light. The devoted energetic work of the united peoples, occidentals and orientals, will succeed in establishing this result, for the force of the Holy Spirit will aid them.

8   The principles of the Teachings of Bahá'u'lláh should be carefully studied, one by one, until they are realized and understood by mind and heart—so will you become strong followers of the light, truly spiritual, heavenly soldiers of God, acquiring and spreading the true civilization in Persia, in Europe, and in the whole world.

9   This will be the paradise which is to come on earth, when all mankind will be gathered together under the tent of unity in the Kingdom of Glory.

5

GOD COMPREHENDS ALL; HE CANNOT BE COMPREHENDED

Friday evening, October 20th

'Abdu'l-Bahá said:

Numerous meetings are held in Paris every day for different purposes, to discuss politics, commerce, education, art, science and many other subjects. 1

All these meetings are good: but *this* assembly has met together to turn their faces towards God, to learn how best to work for the good of humanity, to seek how prejudices may be abolished, and the seed of love and universal brotherhood sown in the heart of man. 2

God approves of the motive of our gathering together and gives us His blessing. 3

In the Old Testament we read that God said, "Let us make man in Our own image." In the Gospel, Christ said, "I am in the Father, and the Father in Me."* In the Qur'án, God says, "Man is my Mystery and I am his." Bahá'u'lláh writes that God 4

---

* John 14:11.

15

says, "Thy heart is My home; purify it for My descent. Thy spirit is My place of revelation; cleanse it for My manifestation."

5   All these sacred words show us that man is made in God's image: yet the Essence of God is incomprehensible to the human mind, for the finite understanding cannot be applied to this infinite Mystery. God contains all: He cannot be contained. That which contains is superior to that which is contained. The whole is greater than its parts.

6   Things which are understood by men cannot be outside their capacity for understanding, so that it is impossible for the heart of man to comprehend the nature of the Majesty of God. Our imagination can only picture that which it is able to create.

7   The power of the understanding differs in degree in the various kingdoms of creation. The mineral, vegetable, and animal realms are each incapable of understanding any creation beyond their own. The mineral cannot imagine the growing power of the plant. The tree cannot understand the power of movement in the animal, neither can it comprehend what it would mean to possess sight, hearing or the sense of smell. These all belong to the physical creation.

8   Man also shares in this creation; but it is not possible for either of the lower kingdoms to understand that which takes place in the mind of man. The animal cannot realize the intelligence of a human being, he only knows that which is perceived by his animal senses, he cannot imagine anything in the abstract. An animal could not learn that the world is round, that the earth revolves round the sun, or the construction of the electric telegraph. These things are only possible to man. Man is the highest work of creation, the nearest to God of all creatures.

All superior kingdoms are incomprehensible to the inferior;   9
how therefore could it be possible that the creature, man,
should understand the almighty Creator of all?

That which we imagine, is not the Reality of God; He,   10
the Unknowable, the Unthinkable, is far beyond the highest
conception of man.

All creatures that exist are dependent upon the Divine   11
Bounty. Divine Mercy gives life itself. As the light of the
sun shines on the whole world, so the Mercy of the infinite
God is shed on all creatures. As the sun ripens the fruits of
the earth, and gives life and warmth to all living beings, so
shines the Sun of Truth on all souls, filling them with the fire
of Divine love and understanding.

The superiority of man over the rest of the created world is   12
seen again in this, that man has a soul in which dwells the divine
spirit; the souls of the lower creatures are inferior in their essence.

There is no doubt then, that of all created beings man is   13
the nearest to the nature of God, and therefore receives a
greater gift of the Divine Bounty.

The mineral kingdom possesses the power of existing. The   14
plant has the power of existing and growing. The animal, in
addition to existence and growth, has the capacity of moving
about, and the use of the faculties of the senses. In the human
kingdom we find all the attributes of the lower worlds, with
much more added thereto. Man is the sum of every previous
creation, for he contains them all.

To man is given the special gift of the intellect by which   15
he is able to receive a larger share of the light Divine. The
Perfect Man is as a polished mirror reflecting the Sun of Truth,
manifesting the attributes of God.

16   The Lord Christ said, "He that hath seen Me hath seen the Father"—God manifested in man.

17   The sun does not leave his place in the heavens and descend into the mirror, for the actions of ascent and descent, coming and going, do not belong to the Infinite, they are the methods of finite beings. In the Manifestation of God, the perfectly polished mirror, appear the qualities of the Divine in a form that man is capable of comprehending.

18   This is so simple that all can understand it, and that which we are able to understand we must perforce accept.

19   Our Father will not hold us responsible for the rejection of dogmas which we are unable either to believe or comprehend, for He is ever infinitely just to His children.

20   This example is, however, so logical that it can easily be grasped by all minds willing to give it their consideration.

21   May each one of you become a shining lamp, of which the flame is the Love of God. May your hearts burn with the radiance of unity. May your eyes be illumined with the effulgence of the Sun of Truth!

22   The city of Paris is very beautiful, a more civilized and well-appointed town in all material development it would be impossible to find in the present world. But the spiritual light has not shone upon her for a long time: her spiritual progress is far behind that of her material civilization. A supreme power is needed to awaken her to the reality of spiritual truth, to breathe the breath of life into her dormant soul. You must all unite in this work of arousing her, in reanimating her people by the help of that Superior Force.

23   When an illness is slight a small remedy will suffice to heal it, but when the slight illness becomes a terrible disease, then a very strong remedy must be used by the Divine Healer.

There are some trees that blossom and bear fruit in a cool climate, others there are which need the hottest rays of the sun to bring them to perfect maturity. Paris is one of those trees for whose spiritual unfoldment a great flaming Sun of the Divine Power of God is needed.

I ask you all, each one of you, to follow well the light of truth, in the Holy Teachings, and God will strengthen you by His Holy Spirit so that you will be enabled to overcome the difficulties, and to destroy the prejudices which cause separation and hatred amongst the people. Let your hearts be filled with the great love of God, let it be felt by all; for every man is a servant of God, and all are entitled to a share of the Divine Bounty. 24

Especially to those whose thoughts are material and retrograde show the utmost love and patience, thereby winning them into the unity of fellowship by the radiance of your kindness. 25

If you are faithful to your great work, following the Holy Sun of Truth without swerving, then will the blessed day of universal brotherhood dawn on this beautiful city. 26

6

THE PITIFUL CAUSES OF WAR, AND THE DUTY OF EVERYONE TO STRIVE FOR PEACE

October 21st

'Abdu'l-Bahá said:

I hope you are all happy and well. I am not happy, but very sad. The news of the Battle of Benghazi grieves my heart. I wonder at the human savagery that still exists in the world! How is it possible for men to fight from morning until evening, killing each other, shedding the blood of their fellowmen: And for what object? To gain possession of a part of the earth! Even the animals, when they fight, have an immediate and more reasonable cause for their attacks! How terrible it is that men, who are of the higher kingdom, can descend to slaying and bringing misery to their fellow-beings, for the possession of a tract of land!

The highest of created beings fighting to obtain the lowest form of matter, earth! Land belongs not to one people, but to all people. This earth is not man's home, but his tomb. It is for their tombs these men are fighting. There is noth-

21

ing so horrible in this world as the tomb, the abode of the decaying bodies of men.

3 However great the conqueror, however many countries he may reduce to slavery, he is unable to retain any part of these devastated lands but one tiny portion—his tomb! If more land is required for the improvement of the condition of the people, for the spread of civilization (for the substitution of just laws for brutal customs)—surely it would be possible to acquire peaceably the necessary extension of territory.

4 But war is made for the satisfaction of men's ambition; for the sake of worldly gain to the few, terrible misery is brought to numberless homes, breaking the hearts of hundreds of men and women!

5 How many widows mourn their husbands, how many stories of savage cruelty do we hear! How many little orphaned children are crying for their dead fathers, how many women are weeping for their slain sons!

6 There is nothing so heartbreaking and terrible as an outburst of human savagery!

7 I charge you all that each one of you concentrate all the thoughts of your heart on love and unity. When a thought of war comes, oppose it by a stronger thought of peace. A thought of hatred must be destroyed by a more powerful thought of love. Thoughts of war bring destruction to all harmony, well-being, restfulness and content.

8 Thoughts of love are constructive of brotherhood, peace, friendship, and happiness.

9 When soldiers of the world draw their swords to kill, soldiers of God clasp each other's hands! So may all the savagery of man disappear by the Mercy of God, working through the

pure in heart and the sincere of soul. Do not think the peace of the world an ideal impossible to attain!

Nothing is impossible to the Divine Benevolence of God. 10

If you desire with all your heart, friendship with every race 11 on earth, your thought, spiritual and positive, will spread; it will become the desire of others, growing stronger and stronger, until it reaches the minds of all men.

Do not despair! Work steadily. Sincerity and love will con- 12 quer hate. How many seemingly impossible events are coming to pass in these days! Set your faces steadily towards the Light of the World. Show love to all; "Love is the breath of the Holy Spirit in the heart of Man." Take courage! God never forsakes His children who strive and work and pray! Let your hearts be filled with the strenuous desire that tranquillity and harmony may encircle all this warring world. So will success crown your efforts, and with the universal brotherhood will come the Kingdom of God in peace and goodwill.

In this room today are members of many races, French, 13 American, English, German, Italian, brothers and sisters meeting in friendship and harmony! Let this gathering be a foreshadowing of what will, in very truth, take place in this world, when every child of God realizes that they are leaves of one tree, flowers in one garden, drops in one ocean, and sons and daughters of one Father, whose name is love!

7

THE SUN OF TRUTH

October 22nd

'Abdu'l-Bahá said:

It is a lovely day, the sun shines brightly upon the earth,   1
giving light and warmth to all creatures. The Sun of Truth
is also shining, giving light and warmth to the souls of men.
The sun is the life-giver to the physical bodies of all creatures upon earth; without its warmth their growth would be
stunted, their development would be arrested, they would
decay and die. Even so do the souls of men need the Sun of
Truth to shed its rays upon their souls, to develop them, to
educate and encourage them. As the sun is to the body of a
man so is the Sun of Truth to his soul.

A man may have attained to a high degree of material   2
progress, but without the light of truth his soul is stunted
and starved. Another man may have no material gifts, may
be at the bottom of the social ladder, but, having received the
warmth of the Sun of Truth his soul is great and his spiritual
understanding is enlightened.

A Greek philosopher living in the days of the youth of   3
Christianity, being full of the Christian element, though not a

professing Christian, wrote thus: "It is my belief that religion is the very foundation of true civilization." For, unless the moral character of a nation is educated, as well as its brain and its talents, civilization has no sure basis.

4   As religion inculcates morality, it is therefore the truest philosophy, and on it is built the only lasting civilization. As an example of this, he points out the Christians of the time whose morality was on a very high level. The belief of this philosopher conforms to the truth, for the civilization of Christianity was the best and most enlightened in the world. The Christian Teaching was illumined by the Divine Sun of Truth, therefore its followers were taught to love all men as brothers to fear nothing, not even death! To love their neighbors as themselves, and to forget their own selfish interests in striving for the greater good of humanity. The grand aim of the religion of Christ was to draw the hearts of all men nearer to God's effulgent Truth.

5   If the followers of the Lord Christ had continued to follow out these principles with steadfast faithfulness, there would have been no need for a renewal of the Christian Message, no necessity for a reawakening of His people, for a great and glorious civilization would now be ruling the world and the Kingdom of Heaven would have come on earth.

6   But instead of this, what has taken place! Men turned away their faces from following the divinely illuminated precepts of their Master, and winter fell upon the hearts of men. For, as the body of man depends for life upon the rays of the sun, so cannot the celestial virtues grow in the soul without the radiance of the Sun of Truth.

7   God leaves not His children comfortless, but, when the darkness of winter overshadows them, then again He sends

His Messengers, the Prophets, with a renewal of the blessed spring. The Sun of Truth appears again on the horizon of the world shining into the eyes of those who sleep, awaking them to behold the glory of a new dawn. Then again will the tree of humanity blossom and bring forth the fruit of righteousness for the healing of the nations. Because man has stopped his ears to the Voice of Truth and shut his eyes to the Sacred Light, neglecting the Law of God, for this reason has the darkness of war and tumult, unrest and misery, desolated the earth. I pray that you will all strive to bring each child of God into the radiance of the Sun of Truth, that the darkness may be dissipated by the penetrating rays of its glory, and the winter's hardness and cold may be melted away by the merciful warmth of its shining.

8

THE LIGHT OF TRUTH
IS NOW SHINING UPON
THE EAST AND THE WEST

Monday, October 23rd

When a man has found the joy of life in one place, he returns 1
to that same spot to find more joy. When a man has found gold
in a mine, he returns again to that mine to dig for more gold.

This shows the internal force and natural instinct which 2
God has given to man, and the power of vital energy which
is born in him.

The West has always received spiritual enlightenment from 3
the East. The Song of the Kingdom is first heard in the East,
but in the West the greater volume of sound bursts upon the
listening ears.

The Lord Christ arose as a bright Star in the Eastern sky, but 4
the light of His Teaching shone more perfectly in the West,
where His influence has taken root more firmly and His Cause
has spread to a greater degree than in the land of His birth.

The sound of the Song of Christ has echoed over all the 5
lands of the Western World and entered the hearts of its
people.

6   The people of the West are firm, and the foundations on which they build are of rock; they are steadfast, and do not easily forget.

7   The West is like a strong sturdy plant; when the rain falls gently upon it to give it nourishment and the sun shines upon it, then does it blossom in due time and bring forth good fruit. It is a long time since the Sun of Truth mirrored forth by the Lord Christ has shed its radiance upon the West, for the Face of God has been veiled by the sin and forgetfulness of man. But now again, praise be to God, the Holy Spirit speaks anew to the world! The constellation of love and wisdom and power is once more shining from the Divine Horizon to give joy to all who turn their faces to the Light of God. Bahá'u'lláh has rent the veil of prejudice and superstition which was stifling the souls of men. Let us pray to God that the breath of the Holy Spirit may again give hope and refreshment to the people, awakening in them a desire to do the Will of God. May heart and soul be vivified in every man: so will they all rejoice in a new birth.

8   Then shall humanity put on a new garment in the radiance of the love of God, and it shall be the dawn of a new creation! Then will the Mercy of the Most Merciful be showered upon all mankind and they will arise to a new life.

9   My earnest desire is that you will all strive and work for this glorious end; that you will be faithful and loving workers in the building of the new spiritual civilization; the elect of God, in willing joyful obedience carrying out His supreme design! Success is truly near at hand, for the Flag of Divinity has been raised aloft, and the Sun of the Righteousness of God appeareth upon the horizon in the sight of all men!

9

THE UNIVERSAL LOVE

October 24th

An Indian said to 'Abdu'l-Bahá:

"My aim in life is to transmit as far as in me lies the message of Krishna to the world."

'Abdu'l-Bahá said: The Message of Krishna is the message   1
of love. All God's prophets have brought the message of love.
None has ever thought that war and hate are good. Everyone
agrees in saying that love and kindness are best.

Love manifests its reality in deeds, not only in words—these   2
alone are without effect. In order that love may manifest its
power there must be an object, an instrument, a motive.

There are many ways of expressing the love principle; there   3
is love for the family, for the country, for the race, there is
political enthusiasm, there is also the love of community of
interest in service. These are all ways and means of showing
the power of love. Without any such means, love would be
unseen, unheard, unfelt—altogether unexpressed, unmanifested! Water shows its power in various ways, in quenching
thirst, causing seed to grow, etc. Coal expresses one of its
principles in gaslight, while one of the powers of electricity
is shown in the electric light. If there were neither gas nor

electricity, the nights of the world would be darkness! So, it is necessary to have an instrument, a motive for love's manifestation, an object, a mode of expression.

4 We must find a way of spreading love among the sons of humanity.

5 Love is unlimited, boundless, infinite! Material things are limited, circumscribed, finite. You cannot adequately express infinite love by limited means.

6 The perfect love needs an unselfish instrument, absolutely freed from fetters of every kind. The love of family is limited; the tie of blood relationship is not the strongest bond. Frequently members of the same family disagree, and even hate each other.

7 Patriotic love is finite; the love of one's country causing hatred of all others, is not perfect love! Compatriots also are not free from quarrels amongst themselves.

8 The love of race is limited; there is some union here, but that is insufficient. Love must be free from boundaries!

9 To love our own race may mean hatred of all others, and even people of the same race often dislike each other.

10 Political love also is much bound up with hatred of one party for another; this love is very limited and uncertain.

11 The love of community of interest in service is likewise fluctuating; frequently competitions arise, which lead to jealousy, and at length hatred replaces love.

12 A few years ago, Turkey and Italy had a friendly political understanding; now they are at war!

13 All these ties of love are imperfect. It is clear that limited material ties are insufficient to adequately express the universal love.

14 The great unselfish love for humanity is bounded by none of these imperfect, semi-selfish bonds; this is the one perfect

love, possible to all mankind, and can only be achieved by the power of the Divine Spirit. No worldly power can accomplish the universal love.

Let all be united in this Divine power of love! Let all 15 strive to grow in the light of the Sun of Truth, and reflecting this luminous love on all men, may their hearts become so united that they may dwell evermore in the radiance of the limitless love.

Remember these words which I speak unto you during 16 the short time I am amongst you in Paris. I earnestly exhort you: let not your hearts be fettered by the material things of this world; I charge you not to lie contentedly on the beds of negligence, prisoners of matter, but to arise and free yourselves from its chains!

The animal creation is captive to matter, God has given 17 freedom to man. The animal cannot escape the law of nature, whereas man may control it, for he, containing nature, can rise above it.

The power of the Holy Spirit, enlightening man's intel- 18 ligence, has enabled him to discover means of bending many natural laws to his will. He flies through the air, floats on the sea, and even moves under the waters.

All this proves how man's intelligence has been enabled to 19 free him from the limitations of nature, and to solve many of her mysteries. Man, to a certain extent, has broken the chains of matter.

The Holy Spirit will give to man greater powers than these, 20 if only he will strive after the things of the spirit and endeavor to attune his heart to the Divine infinite love.

When you love a member of your family or a compatriot, 21 let it be with a ray of the Infinite Love! Let it be in God, and for God! Wherever you find the attributes of God love that person, whether he be of your family or of another. Shed the light of a boundless love on every human being whom you meet, whether of your country, your race, your political party, or of any other nation, color or shade of political opinion. Heaven will support you while you work in this ingathering of the scattered peoples of the world beneath the shadow of the almighty tent of unity.

22   You will be servants of God, who are dwelling near to Him, His divine helpers in the service, ministering to all Humanity. *All* Humanity! Every human being! *Never forget this!*

23   Do not say, he is an Italian, or a Frenchman, or an American, or an Englishman, remember only that he is a son of God, a servant of the Most High, a man! All are *men!* Forget nationalities; *all are equal* in the sight of God!

24   Remember not your own limitations; the help of God will come to you. Forget yourself. God's help will surely come!

25   When you call on the Mercy of God waiting to reinforce you, your strength will be tenfold.

26   Look at me: I am so feeble, yet I have had the strength given me to come amongst you: a poor servant of God, who has been enabled to give you this message! I shall not be with you long! One must never consider one's own feebleness, it is the strength of the Holy Spirit of Love, which gives the power to teach. The thought of our own weakness could only bring despair. We must look higher than all earthly thoughts; detach ourselves from every material idea, crave for the things of the spirit; fix our eyes on the everlasting bountiful Mercy of the Almighty, who will fill our souls with the gladness of joyful service to His command "Love One Another."

10

THE IMPRISONMENT OF 'ABDU'L-BAHÁ

4 Avenue de Camoëns,
Wednesday, October 25th

I regret much that I have kept you waiting this morning, but 1
I have so much to do in a short time for the Cause of the
love of God.

You will not mind having waited a little to see me. I have 2
waited years and years in prison, that I might come to see
you now.

Above all, God be praised, our hearts are always in uni- 3
son, and with one aim are drawn to the love of God. By the
Bounty of the Kingdom our desires, our hearts, our spirits,
are they not united in one bond? Our prayers, are they not
for the gathering together of all men in harmony? Therefore
are we not always together?

Yesterday evening when I came home from the house of 4
Monsieur Dreyfus I was very tired—yet I did not sleep, I lay
awake thinking.

I said, O God, Here am I in Paris! What is Paris and who 5
am I? Never did I dream that from the darkness of my prison

35

I should ever be able to come to you, though when they read me my sentence I did not believe in it.

6   They told me that 'Abdu'l-Ḥamíd had ordered my everlasting imprisonment, and I said, "This is impossible! I shall not always be a prisoner. If 'Abdu'l-Ḥamíd were immortal, such a sentence might possibly be carried out. It is certain that one day I shall be free. My body may be captive for a time, but 'Abdu'l-Ḥamíd has no power over my spirit—free it must remain—*that* can no man imprison."

7   Released from my prison by the Power of God I meet here the friends of God, and I am thankful unto Him.

8   Let us spread the Cause of God, for which I suffered persecution.

9   What a privilege it is for us to meet here in freedom. How happy for us that God has so decided that we may work together for the coming of the Kingdom!

10   Are you pleased to receive such a guest, freed from his prison to bring the glorious Message to you? He who never could have thought such a meeting possible! Now by the Grace of God, by His wonderful Power, I, who was condemned to perpetual imprisonment in a far off town of the East, am here in Paris talking with you!

11   Henceforward we shall always be together, heart and soul and spirit, pressing forward in the work till all men are gathered together under the tent of the Kingdom, singing the songs of peace.

11

GOD'S GREATEST GIFT TO MAN

Thursday, October 26th

God's greatest gift to man is that of intellect, or understanding.   1

The understanding is the power by which man acquires his   2
knowledge of the several kingdoms of creation, and of various
stages of existence, as well as of much which is invisible.

Possessing this gift, he is, in himself, the sum of earlier   3
creations—he is able to get into touch with those kingdoms;
and by this gift, he can frequently, through his scientific
knowledge, reach out with prophetic vision.

Intellect is, in truth, the most precious gift bestowed upon   4
man by the Divine Bounty. Man alone, among created beings,
has this wonderful power.

All creation, preceding Man, is bound by the stern law of   5
nature. The great sun, the multitudes of stars, the oceans and
seas, the mountains, the rivers, the trees, and all animals, great
or small—none is able to evade obedience to nature's law.

Man alone has freedom, and, by his understanding or   6
intellect, has been able to gain control of and adapt some of
those natural laws to his own needs. By the power of his intel-

lect he has discovered means by which he not only traverses great continents in express trains and crosses vast oceans in ships, but, like the fish he travels under water in submarines, and, imitating the birds, he flies through the air in airships.

7   Man has succeeded in using electricity in several ways—for light, for motive power, for sending messages from one end of the earth to the other—and by electricity he can even hear a voice many miles away!

8   By this gift of understanding or intellect he has also been able to use the rays of the sun to picture people and things, and even to capture the form of distant heavenly bodies.

9   We perceive in what numerous ways man has been able to bend the powers of nature to his will.

10   How grievous it is to see how man has used his God-given gift to frame instruments of war, for breaking the Commandment of God "Thou shalt not kill," and for defying Christ's injunction to "Love one another."

11   God gave this power to man that it might be used for the advancement of civilization, for the good of humanity, to increase love and concord and peace. But man prefers to use this gift to destroy instead of to build, for injustice and oppression, for hatred and discord and devastation, for the destruction of his fellow-creatures, whom Christ has commanded that he should love as himself!

12   I hope that you will use *your* understanding to promote the unity and tranquillity of mankind, to give enlightenment and civilization to the people, to produce love in all around you, and to bring about the universal peace.

13   Study the sciences, acquire more and more knowledge. Assuredly one may learn to the end of one's life! Use your knowledge always for the benefit of others; so may war cease

on the face of this beautiful earth, and a glorious edifice of peace and concord be raised. Strive that your high ideals may be realized in the Kingdom of God on earth, as they will be in Heaven.

12

THE CLOUDS THAT OBSCURE THE SUN OF TRUTH

4 Avenue de Camoëns,
Morning of Friday, October 27th

The day is fine, the air is pure, the sun shines, no mist nor cloud obscures its radiance.   1

These brilliant rays penetrate into all parts of the city; so may the Sun of Truth illumine the minds of men.   2

Christ said, "They shall see the Son of Man coming in the clouds of Heaven."* Bahá'u'lláh said, "When Christ came for the first time He came upon the clouds."† Christ said that He had come from the sky, from Heaven—that He came forth from God—while He was born of Mary, His Mother. But when He declared that He had come from Heaven, it is clear that He did not mean the blue firmament but that He spoke of the Heaven of the Kingdom of God, and that from this Heaven He descended upon the clouds. As clouds   3

---

* Matthew 24:30, 16:27.
† John 3:13.

are obstacles to the shining of the sun, so the clouds of the world of humanity hid from the eyes of men the radiance of the Divinity of Christ.

4   Men said, "He is of Nazareth, born of Mary, we know Him and we know His brethren. What can He mean? What is He saying? That He came forth from God?"

5   The Body of Christ was born of Mary of Nazareth, but the Spirit was of God. The capacities of His human body were limited but the strength of His spirit was vast, infinite, immeasurable.

6   Men asked, "Why does He say He is of God?" If they had understood the reality of Christ, they would have known that the body of His humanity was a cloud that hid His Divinity. The world only saw His human form, and therefore wondered how He could have "come down from Heaven."

7   Bahá'u'lláh said, "Even as the clouds hide the sun and the sky from our gaze, even so did the humanity of Christ hide from men His real Divine character."

8   I hope that you will turn with unclouded eyes towards the Sun of Truth, beholding not the things of earth, lest your hearts be attracted to the worthless and passing pleasures of the world; let that Sun give you of His strength, then will not the clouds of prejudice veil His illumination from your eyes! Then will the Sun be without clouds for you.

9   Breathe the air of purity. May you each and all share in the Divine Bounties of the Kingdom of Heaven. May the world be for you no obstacle hiding the truth from your sight, as the human body of Christ hid His Divinity from the people of His day. May you receive the clear vision of the Holy Spirit, so that your hearts may be illumined and able

to recognize the Sun of Truth shining through all material clouds, His splendor flooding the universe.

Let not the things of the body obscure the celestial light of   10
the spirit, so that, by the Divine Bounty, you may enter with the children of God into His Eternal Kingdom.

This is my prayer for you all.   11

13

RELIGIOUS PREJUDICES

October 27th

The basis of the teaching of Bahá'u'lláh is the *Unity of* 1
Mankind, and His greatest desire was that love and goodwill
should live in the heart of men.

As He exhorted the people to do away with strife and dis- 2
cord, so I wish to explain to you the principal reason of the
unrest among nations. The chief cause is the misrepresenta-
tion of religion by the religious leaders and teachers. They
teach their followers to believe that their own form of religion
is the only one pleasing to God, and that followers of any
other persuasion are condemned by the All-Loving Father
and deprived of His Mercy and Grace. Hence arise among
the peoples, disapproval, contempt, disputes and hatred. If
these religious prejudices could be swept away, the nations
would soon enjoy peace and concord.

I was once at Tiberias where the Jews have a Temple. I was 3
staying in a house just opposite the Temple, and there I saw
and heard a Rabbi speaking to his congregation of Jews, and
he spoke thus:

4   "O Jews, you are in truth the people of God! All other races and religions are of the devil. God has created you the descendants of Abraham, and He has showered His blessings upon you. Unto you God sent Moses, Jacob and Joseph, and many other great prophets. These prophets, one and all, were of your race.

5   "It was for you that God broke the power of Pharaoh and caused the Red Sea to dry up; to you also He sent manna from above to be your food, and out of the stony rock did He give you water to quench your thirst. You are indeed the chosen people of God, you are above all the races of the earth! Therefore, all other races are abhorrent to God, and condemned by Him. In truth you will govern and subdue the world, and all men shall become your slaves.

6   "Do not profane yourselves by consorting with people who are not of your own religion, make not friends of such men."

7   When the Rabbi had finished his eloquent discourse, his hearers were filled with joy and satisfaction. It is impossible to describe to you their happiness!

8   Alas! It is misguided ones like these who are the cause of division and hatred upon earth. Today there are millions of people who still worship idols, and the great religions of the world are at war among themselves. For 1,300 years, Christians and Muslims have been quarreling, when with very little effort their differences and disputes could be overcome and peace and harmony could exist between them and the world could be at rest!

9   In the Qur'án we read that Muḥammad spoke to His followers, saying:

10   "Why do you not believe in Christ, and in the Gospel? Why will you not accept Moses and the Prophets, for surely

the Bible is the Book of God? In truth, Moses was a sublime Prophet, and Jesus was filled with the Holy Spirit. He came to the world through the Power of God, born of the Holy Spirit and of the blessed Virgin Mary. Mary, His mother, was a saint from Heaven. She passed her days in the Temple at prayer and food was sent to her from above. Her father, Zacharias, came to her and asked her from whence the food came, and Mary made answer, 'From on high.' Surely God made Mary to be exalted above all other women."

This is what Muḥammad taught His people concerning   11
Jesus and Moses, and He reproached them for their lack of faith in these great Teachers, and taught them the lessons of truth and tolerance. Muḥammad was sent from God to work among a people as savage and uncivilized as the wild beasts. They were quite devoid of understanding, nor had they any feelings of love, sympathy and pity. Women were so degraded and despised that a man could bury his daughter alive, and he had as many wives to be his slaves as he chose.

Among these half animal people Muḥammad was sent with   12
His divine Message. He taught the people that idol worship was wrong, and that they should reverence Christ, Moses and the Prophets. Under His influence they became a more enlightened and civilized people and arose from the degraded state in which He found them. Was not this a good work, and worthy of all praise, respect and love?

Look at the Gospel of the Lord Christ and see how glori-   13
ous it is! Yet even today men fail to understand its priceless beauty, and misinterpret its words of wisdom.

Christ forbade war! When the disciple Peter, thinking to   14
defend his Lord, cut off the ear of the servant of the High

Priest, Christ said to him: "Put up thy sword into the sheath."*
Yet, in spite of the direct command of the Lord they profess
to serve—men still dispute, make war, and kill one another,
and His counsels and teaching seem quite forgotten.

15   But do not therefore attribute to the Masters and Prophets
the evil deeds of their followers. If the priests, teachers and
people, lead lives which are contrary to the religion they profess to follow, is that the fault of Christ or the other Teachers?

16   The people of Islám were taught to realize how Jesus came from
God and was born of the Spirit, and that He must be glorified of
all men. Moses was a prophet of God, and revealed in His day and
for the people to whom He was sent, the Book of God.

17   Muḥammad recognized the sublime grandeur of Christ and the
greatness of Moses and the prophets. If only the whole world would
acknowledge the greatness of Muḥammad and all the Heaven-sent
Teachers, strife and discord would soon vanish from the face of
the earth, and God's Kingdom would come among men.

18   The people of Islám who glorify Christ are not humiliated
by so doing.

19   Christ was the Prophet of the Christians, Moses of the
Jews—why should not the followers of each prophet recognize
and honor the other prophets also? If men could only learn the
lesson of mutual tolerance, understanding, and brotherly love,
the unity of the world would soon be an established fact.

20   Bahá'u'lláh spent His life teaching this lesson of Love and
Unity. Let us then put away from us all prejudice and intoler-
ance, and strive with all our hearts and souls to bring about
understanding and unity between Christians and Muslims.

---

* John 18:11.

14

THE BENEFITS OF
GOD TO MAN

4 Avenue de Camoëns,
October 27th

God alone ordereth all things and is all-powerful. Why then 1
does He send trials to His servants?

The trials of man are of two kinds. (a) The consequences 2
of his own actions. If a man eats too much, he ruins his digestion; if he takes poison he becomes ill or dies. If a person
gambles he will lose his money; if he drinks too much he will
lose his equilibrium. All these sufferings are caused by the
man himself, it is quite clear therefore that certain sorrows
are the result of our own deeds.

(b) Other sufferings there are, which come upon the Faith- 3
ful of God. Consider the great sorrows endured by Christ
and by His apostles!

Those who suffer most, attain to the greatest perfection. 4

Those who declare a wish to suffer much for Christ's sake 5
must prove their sincerity; those who proclaim their longing
to make great sacrifices can only prove their truth by their
deeds. Job proved the fidelity of his love for God by being

faithful through his great adversity, as well as during the prosperity of his life. The apostles of Christ who steadfastly bore all their trials and sufferings—did they not prove their faithfulness? Was not their endurance the best proof?

6   These griefs are now ended.

7   Caiaphas lived a comfortable and happy life while Peter's life was full of sorrow and trial; which of these two is the more enviable? Assuredly we should choose the present state of Peter, for he possesses immortal life whilst Caiaphas has won eternal shame. The trials of Peter tested his fidelity. Tests are benefits from God, for which we should thank Him. Grief and sorrow do not come to us by chance, they are sent to us by the Divine Mercy for our own perfecting.

8   While a man is happy he may forget his God; but when grief comes and sorrows overwhelm him, then will he remember his Father who is in Heaven, and who is able to deliver him from his humiliations.

9   Men who suffer not, attain no perfection. The plant most pruned by the gardeners is that one which, when the summer comes, will have the most beautiful blossoms and the most abundant fruit.

10   The laborer cuts up the earth with his plough, and from that earth comes the rich and plentiful harvest. The more a man is chastened, the greater is the harvest of spiritual virtues shown forth by him. A soldier is no good General until he has been in the front of the fiercest battle and has received the deepest wounds.

11   The prayer of the prophets of God has always been, and still is: Oh God, I long to lay down my life in the path to Thee! I desire to shed my blood for Thee, and to make the supreme sacrifice.

15

BEAUTY AND HARMONY IN DIVERSITY

October 28th

The Creator of all is One God.   1

From this same God all creation sprang into existence, and   2
He is the one goal, towards which everything in nature yearns.
This conception was embodied in the words of Christ, when
He said, "I am the Alpha and the Omega, the beginning and
the end." Man is the sum of Creation, and the Perfect Man is
the expression of the complete thought of the Creator—the
Word of God.

Consider the world of created beings, how varied and   3
diverse they are in species, yet with one sole origin. All the
differences that appear are those of outward form and color.
This diversity of type is apparent throughout the whole of
nature.

Behold a beautiful garden full of flowers, shrubs, and   4
trees. Each flower has a different charm, a peculiar beauty,
its own delicious perfume and beautiful color. The trees too,
how varied are they in size, in growth, in foliage—and what
different fruits they bear! Yet all these flowers, shrubs and

trees spring from the self-same earth, the same sun shines upon them and the same clouds give them rain.

5   So it is with humanity. It is made up of many races, and its peoples are of different color, white, black, yellow, brown and red—but they all come from the same God, and all are servants to Him. This diversity among the children of men has unhappily not the same effect as it has among the vegetable creation, where the spirit shown is more harmonious. Among men exists the diversity of animosity, and it is this that causes war and hatred among the different nations of the world.

6   Differences which are only those of blood also cause them to destroy and kill one another. Alas! that this should still be so. Let *us* look rather at the beauty in diversity, the beauty of harmony, and learn a lesson from the vegetable creation. If you beheld a garden in which all the plants were the same as to form, color and perfume, it would not seem beautiful to you at all, but, rather, monotonous and dull. The garden which is pleasing to the eye and which makes the heart glad, is the garden in which are growing side by side flowers of every hue, form and perfume, and the joyous contrast of color is what makes for charm and beauty. So is it with trees. An orchard full of fruit trees is a delight; so is a plantation planted with many species of shrubs. It is just the diversity and variety that constitutes its charm; each flower, each tree, each fruit, beside being beautiful in itself, brings out by contrast the qualities of the others, and shows to advantage the special loveliness of each and all.

7   Thus should it be among the children of men! The diversity in the human family should be the cause of love and harmony, as it is in music where many different notes blend together in the making of a perfect chord. If you meet those

of different race and color from yourself, do not mistrust them and withdraw yourself into your shell of conventionality, but rather be glad and show them kindness. Think of them as different colored roses growing in the beautiful garden of humanity, and rejoice to be among them.

Likewise, when you meet those whose opinions differ from your own, do not turn away your face from them. All are seeking truth, and there are many roads leading thereto. Truth has many aspects, but it remains always and forever one. 8

Do not allow difference of opinion, or diversity of thought to separate you from your fellowmen, or to be the cause of dispute, hatred and strife in your hearts. 9

Rather, search diligently for the truth and make all men your friends. 10

Every edifice is made of many different stones, yet each depends on the other to such an extent that if one were displaced the whole building would suffer; if one is faulty the structure is imperfect. 11

Bahá'u'lláh has drawn the circle of unity, He has made a design for the uniting of all the peoples, and for the gathering of them all under the shelter of the tent of universal unity. This is the work of the Divine Bounty, and we must all strive with heart and soul until we have the reality of unity in our midst, and as we work, so will strength be given unto us. Leave all thought of self, and strive only to be obedient and submissive to the Will of God. In this way only shall we become citizens of the Kingdom of God, and attain unto life everlasting. 12

16

THE TRUE MEANING OF THE PROPHECIES CONCERNING THE COMING OF CHRIST

October 30th

In the Bible there are prophecies of the coming of Christ. 1
The Jews still await the coming of the Messiah, and pray to God day and night to hasten His advent.

When Christ came they denounced and slew Him, say- 2
ing: "This is not the One for whom we wait. Behold when the Messiah shall come, signs and wonders shall testify that He is in truth the Christ. We know the signs and conditions, and they have not appeared. The Messiah will arise out of an unknown city. He shall sit upon the throne of David, and behold, He shall come with a sword of steel, and with a scepter of iron shall He rule! He shall fulfill the law of the Prophets, He shall conquer the East and the West, and shall glorify His chosen people the Jews. He shall bring with Him a reign of peace, during which even the animals shall cease to be at enmity with man. For behold the wolf and the lamb shall drink from the same spring, and the lion and the doe shall lie

down in the same pasture, the serpent and the mouse shall share the same nest, and all God's creatures shall be at rest."

3   According to the Jews, Jesus the Christ fulfilled none of these conditions, for their eyes were holden and they could not see.

4   He came from Nazareth, no unknown place. He carried no sword in His hand, nor even a stick. He did not sit upon the Throne of David, He was a poor man. He reformed the Law of Moses, and broke the Sabbath Day. He did not conquer the East and the West, but was Himself subject to the Roman Law. He did not exalt the Jews, but taught equality and brotherhood, and rebuked the Scribes and Pharisees. He brought in no reign of peace, for during His lifetime injustice and cruelty reached such a height that even He Himself fell a victim to it, and died a shameful death upon the cross.

5   Thus the Jews thought and spoke, for they did not understand the Scriptures nor the glorious truths that were contained in them. The letter they knew by heart, but of the life-giving spirit they understood not a word.

6   Hearken, and I will show you the meaning thereof. Although He came from Nazareth, which was a known place, He also came from Heaven. His body was born of Mary, but His Spirit came from Heaven. The sword He carried was the sword of His tongue, with which He divided the good from the evil, the true from the false, the faithful from the unfaithful, and the light from the darkness. His Word was indeed a sharp sword! The Throne upon which He sat is the Eternal Throne from which Christ reigns forever, a heavenly throne, not an earthly one, for the things of earth pass away but heavenly things pass not away. He reinterpreted and completed the Law of Moses and fulfilled the Law of the Prophets. His word

conquered the East and the West. His Kingdom is everlasting. He exalted those Jews who recognized Him. They were men and women of humble birth, but contact with Him made them great and gave them everlasting dignity. The animals who were to live with one another signified the different sects and races, who, once having been at war, were now to dwell in love and charity, drinking together the water of life from Christ the Eternal Spring.

Thus, all the spiritual prophecies concerning the coming 7 of Christ were fulfilled, but the Jews shut their eyes that they should not see, and their ears that they should not hear, and the Divine Reality of Christ passed through their midst unheard, unloved and unrecognized.

It is easy to read the Holy Scriptures, but it is only with a 8 clean heart and a pure mind that one may understand their true meaning. Let us ask God's help to enable us to understand the Holy Books. Let us pray for eyes to see and ears to hear, and for hearts that long for peace.

God's eternal Mercy is immeasurable. He has always chosen 9 certain souls upon whom He has shed the Divine Bounty of His heart, whose minds He has illumined with celestial light, to whom He has revealed the sacred mysteries, and kept clear before their sight the Mirror of Truth. These are the disciples of God, and His goodness has no bounds. You who are servants of the Most High may be disciples also. The treasuries of God are limitless.

The Spirit breathing through the Holy Scriptures is food 10 for all who hunger. God Who has given the revelation to His Prophets will surely give of His abundance daily bread to all those who ask Him faithfully.

17

THE HOLY SPIRIT, THE INTERMEDIARY POWER BETWEEN GOD AND MAN

4 Avenue de Camoëns,
October 31st

The Divine Reality is Unthinkable, Limitless, Eternal, Immortal and Invisible.   1

The world of creation is bound by natural law, finite and mortal.   2

The Infinite Reality cannot be said to ascend or descend. It is beyond the understanding of man, and cannot be described in terms which apply to the phenomenal sphere of the created world.   3

Man, then, is in extreme need of the only Power by which he is able to receive help from the Divine Reality, that Power alone bringing him into contact with the Source of all life.   4

An intermediary is needed to bring two extremes into relation with each other. Riches and poverty, plenty and need: without an intermediary power there could be no relation between these pairs of opposites.   5

6   So we can say there must be a Mediator between God and Man, and this is none other than the Holy Spirit, which brings the created earth into relation with the "Unthinkable One," the Divine Reality.

7   The Divine Reality may be likened to the sun and the Holy Spirit to the rays of the sun. As the rays of the sun bring the light and warmth of the sun to the earth, giving life to all created beings, so do the "Manifestations"* bring the power of the Holy Spirit from the Divine Sun of Reality to give light and life to the souls of men.

8   Behold, there is an intermediary necessary between the sun and the earth; the sun does not descend to the earth, neither does the earth ascend to the sun. This contact is made by the rays of the sun which bring light and warmth and heat.

9   The Holy Spirit is the Light from the Sun of Truth bringing, by its infinite power, life and illumination to all mankind, flooding all souls with Divine Radiance, conveying the blessings of God's Mercy to the whole world. The earth, without the medium of the warmth and light of the rays of the sun, could receive no benefits from the sun.

10   Likewise the Holy Spirit is the very cause of the life of man; without the Holy Spirit he would have no intellect, he would be unable to acquire his scientific knowledge by which his great influence over the rest of creation is gained. The illumination of the Holy Spirit gives to man the power of thought, and enables him to make discoveries by which he bends the laws of nature to his will.

11   The Holy Spirit it is which, through the mediation of the Prophets of God, teaches spiritual virtues to man and enables him to attain Eternal Life.

---

* Manifestations of God.

All these blessings are brought to man by the Holy Spirit; 12
therefore we can understand that the Holy Spirit is the Intermediary between the Creator and the created. The light
and heat of the sun cause the earth to be fruitful, and create
life in all things that grow; and the Holy Spirit quickens the
souls of men.

The two great apostles, St. Peter and St. John the Evan- 13
gelist, were once simple, humble workmen, toiling for their
daily bread. By the Power of the Holy Spirit their souls were
illumined, and they received the eternal blessings of the Lord
Christ.

18

THE TWO NATURES
IN MAN

November 1st

Today is a day of rejoicing in Paris! They are celebrating the
Festival of "All Saints." Why do you think that these people
were called "Saints?" The word has a very real meaning. A
saint is one who leads a life of purity, one who has freed
himself from all human weaknesses and imperfections.   1

In man there are two natures; his spiritual or higher nature   2
and his material or lower nature. In one he approaches God,
in the other he lives for the world alone. Signs of both these
natures are to be found in men. In his material aspect he
expresses untruth, cruelty and injustice; all these are the outcome of his lower nature. The attributes of his Divine nature
are shown forth in love, mercy, kindness, truth and justice,
one and all being expressions of his higher nature. Every good
habit, every noble quality belongs to man's spiritual nature,
whereas all his imperfections and sinful actions are born of
his material nature. If a man's Divine nature dominates his
human nature, we have a saint.

3   Man has the power both to do good and to do evil; if his power for good predominates and his inclinations to do wrong are conquered, then man in truth may be called a saint. But if, on the contrary, he rejects the things of God and allows his evil passions to conquer him, then he is no better than a mere animal.

4   Saints are men who have freed themselves from the world of matter and who have overcome sin. They live in the world but are not of it, their thoughts being continually in the world of the spirit. Their lives are spent in holiness, and their deeds show forth love, justice and godliness. They are illumined from on high; they are as bright and shining lamps in the dark places of the earth. These are the saints of God. The apostles, who were the disciples of Jesus Christ, were just as other men are; they, like their fellows, were attracted by the things of the world, and each thought only of his own advantage. They knew little of justice, nor were the Divine perfections found in their midst. But when they followed Christ and believed in Him, their ignorance gave place to understanding, cruelty was changed to justice, falsehood to truth, darkness into light. They had been worldly, they became spiritual and divine. They had been children of darkness, they became sons of God, they became saints! Strive therefore to follow in their steps, leaving all worldly things behind, and striving to attain to the Spiritual Kingdom.

5   Pray to God that He may strengthen you in divine virtue, so that you may be as angels in the world, and beacons of light to disclose the mysteries of the Kingdom to those with understanding hearts.

6   God sent His Prophets into the world to teach and enlighten man, to explain to him the mystery of the Power of

the Holy Spirit, to enable him to reflect the light, and so in his turn, to be the source of guidance to others. The Heavenly Books, the Bible, the Qur'án, and the other Holy Writings have been given by God as guides into the paths of Divine virtue, love, justice and peace.

Therefore I say unto you that ye should strive to follow 7 the counsels of these Blessed Books, and so order your lives that ye may, following the examples set before you, become yourselves the saints of the Most High!

19

MATERIAL AND SPIRITUAL PROGRESS

November 2nd

'Abdu'l-Bahá said:

How beautiful the weather is today, the sky is clear, the sun 1
shines, and the heart of man is made glad thereby!

Such bright and beautiful weather gives new life and 2
strength to man, and if he has been sick, he feels once more
in his heart the joyous hope of health renewed. All these gifts
of nature concern the physical side of man, for it is only his
body that can receive material benefits.

If a man is successful in his business, art, or profession he is 3
thereby enabled to increase his physical wellbeing and to give
his body the amount of ease and comfort in which it delights.
All around us today we see how man surrounds himself with
every modern convenience and luxury, and denies nothing to
the physical and material side of his nature. But, take heed,
lest in thinking too earnestly of the things of the body you
forget the things of the soul: for material advantages do not
elevate the spirit of a man. Perfection in worldly things is a joy
to the body of a man but in no wise does it glorify his soul.

4   It may be that a man who has every material benefit, and who lives surrounded by all the greatest comfort modern civilization can give him, is denied the all important gift of the Holy Spirit.

5   It is indeed a good and praiseworthy thing to progress materially, but in so doing, let us not neglect the more important spiritual progress, and close our eyes to the Divine light shining in our midst.

6   Only by improving spiritually as well as materially can we make any real progress, and become perfect beings. It was in order to bring this spiritual life and light into the world that all the great Teachers have appeared. They came so that the Sun of Truth might be manifested, and shine in the hearts of men, and that through its wondrous power men might attain unto Everlasting Light.

7   When the Lord Christ came He spread the light of the Holy Spirit on all around Him, and His disciples and all who received His illumination became enlightened, spiritual beings.

8   It was to manifest this light that Bahá'u'lláh was born, and came into the world. He taught Eternal Truth to men, and shed the rays of Divine Light in all lands.

9   Alas! behold how man disregards this Light. He still goes on his way of darkness, and disunity, and quarrels and fierce war are still rife.

10   He uses material progress to gratify his lust for war, and he makes destructive implements and appliances to destroy his brother man.

11   But let us rather exert ourselves for the attainment of spiritual advantages, for this is the only way of true progress, that which cometh from God and is alone Godly.

I pray for you one and all that you may receive the Bounties   12
of the Holy Spirit; so will you become in truth enlightened,
and progress ever onward and upward to the Kingdom of
God. Then shall your hearts be prepared to receive the glad
tidings, your eyes shall be opened and you will see the Glory
of God; your ears shall be unstopped and you will hear the
call of the Kingdom, and with tongue made eloquent shall
you call men to the realization of the Divine Power and Love
of God!

20

THE EVOLUTION OF MATTER AND DEVELOPMENT OF THE SOUL

November 3rd

Paris is becoming very cold, so cold that I shall soon be obliged   1
to go away, but the warmth of your love still keeps me here.
God willing, I hope to stay among you yet a little while; bodily
cold and heat cannot affect the spirit, for it is warmed by the
fire of the Love of God. When we understand this, we begin
to understand something of our life in the world to come.

God, in His Bounty, has given us a foretaste here, has   2
given us certain proofs of the difference that exists between
body, soul and spirit.

We see that cold, heat, suffering, etc., only concern the   3
body, they do not touch the spirit.

How often do we see a man, poor, sick, miserably clad, and   4
with no means of support, yet spiritually strong. Whatever
his body has to suffer, his spirit is free and well! Again, how
often do we see a rich man, physically strong and healthy,
but with a soul sick unto death.

5   It is quite apparent to the seeing mind that a man's spirit is something very different from his physical body.

6   The spirit is changeless, indestructible. The progress and development of the soul, the joy and sorrow of the soul, are independent of the physical body.

7   If we are caused joy or pain by a friend, if a love prove true or false, it is the soul that is affected. If our dear ones are far from us—it is the soul that grieves, and the grief or trouble of the soul may react on the body.

8   Thus, when the spirit is fed with holy virtues, then is the body joyous; if the soul falls into sin, the body is in torment!

9   When we find truth, constancy, fidelity, and love, we are happy; but if we meet with lying, faithlessness, and deceit, we are miserable.

10   These are all things pertaining to the soul, and are not *bodily* ills. Thus, it is apparent that the soul, even as the body, has its own individuality. But if the body undergoes a change, the spirit need not be touched. When you break a glass on which the sun shines, the glass is broken, but the sun still shines! If a cage containing a bird is destroyed, the bird is unharmed! If a lamp is broken, the flame can still burn bright!

11   The same thing applies to the spirit of man. Though death destroy his body, it has no power over his spirit—this is eternal, everlasting, both birthless and deathless.

12   As to the soul of man after death, it remains in the degree of purity to which it has evolved during life in the physical body, and after it is freed from the body it remains plunged in the ocean of God's Mercy.

13   From the moment the soul leaves the body and arrives in the Heavenly World, its evolution is spiritual, and that evolution is: *The approaching unto God.*

In the physical creation, evolution is from one degree of 14
perfection to another. The mineral passes with its mineral
perfections to the vegetable; the vegetable, with its perfections,
passes to the animal world, and so on to that of humanity.
This world is full of seeming contradictions; in each of these
kingdoms (mineral, vegetable and animal) life exists in its
degree; though when compared to the life in a man, the earth
appears to be dead, yet she, too, lives and has a life of her
own. In this world things live and die, and live again in other
forms of life, but in the world of the spirit it is quite otherwise.

The soul does not evolve from degree to degree as a law—it 15
only evolves nearer to God, by the Mercy and Bounty of God.

It is my earnest prayer that we may all be in the Kingdom 16
of God, and near Him.

21

THE SPIRITUAL MEETINGS
IN PARIS

November 4th

All over Europe today one hears of meetings and assemblies, and societies of all kinds are formed. There are those interested in commerce, science, and politics, and many others. All these are for *material* service, their desire being for the progress and enlightenment of the world of matter. But rarely does a breath from the spirit world breathe upon them. They seem unconscious of the Divine Voice, careless concerning the things of God. But this meeting in Paris is a truly spiritual one. The Divine Breath is poured forth in your midst, the light of the Kingdom is shining in all hearts. The Divine love of God is a power among you, and with souls athirst, ye receive the glad tidings of great joy.

1

You are all met here with one accord, heart drawn to heart, souls overflowing with Divine love, working and longing for the unity of the world.

2

Verily this assembly is a spiritual one! It is like unto a beautiful perfumed garden! On it the Heavenly Sun sheds the golden rays, and the warmth thereof penetrates and glad-

3

dens each waiting heart. The love of Christ, which passeth all knowledge, is among you, the Holy Spirit is your help.

4   Day by day this meeting will grow and become more powerful until gradually its spirit will conquer the whole world!

5   Try with all your hearts to be willing channels for God's Bounty. For I say unto you that He has chosen you to be His messengers of love throughout the world, to be His bearers of spiritual gifts to man, to be the means of spreading unity and concord on the earth. Thank God with all your hearts that such a privilege has been given unto you. For a life devoted to praise is not too long in which to thank God for such a favor.

6   Lift up your hearts above the present and look with eyes of faith into the future! Today the seed is sown, the grain falls upon the earth, but behold the day will come when it shall rise a glorious tree and the branches thereof shall be laden with fruit. Rejoice and be glad that this day has dawned, try to realize its power, for it is indeed wonderful! God has crowned you with honor and in your hearts has He set a radiant star; verily the light thereof shall brighten the whole world!

22

THE TWO KINDS OF LIGHT

November 5th

Today the weather is gloomy and dull! In the East there is   1
continual sunshine, the stars are never veiled, and there are
very few clouds. Light always rises in the East and sends forth
its radiance into the West.

There are two kinds of light. There is the visible light of   2
the sun, by whose aid we can discern the beauties of the world
around us—without this we could see nothing.

Nevertheless, though it is the function of this light to make   3
things visible to us, it cannot give us the *power* to see them
or to understand what their various charms may be, for this
light has no intelligence, no consciousness. It is the light of
the *intellect* which gives us knowledge and understanding,
and without this light the physical eyes would be useless.

This light of the intellect is the highest light that exists,   4
for it is born of the *Light Divine.*

The light of the intellect enables us to understand and   5
realize all that exists, but it is only the Divine Light that can
give us sight for the invisible things, and which enables us

to see truths that will only be visible to the world thousands of years hence.

6 It was the Divine Light which enabled the prophets to see two thousand years in advance what was going to take place and today we see the realization of their vision. Thus it is this Light which we must strive to seek, for it is greater than any other.

7 It was by this Light that Moses was enabled to see and comprehend the Divine Appearance, and to hear the Heavenly Voice which spoke to Him from the Burning Bush.*

8 It is of this Light Muḥammad is speaking when He says, "Alláh is the light of the Heavens, and of the Earth."

9 Seek with all your hearts this Heavenly Light, so that you may be enabled to understand the realities, that you may know the secret things of God, that the hidden ways may be made plain before your eyes.

10 This light may be likened unto a mirror, and as a mirror reflects all that is before it, so this Light shows to the eyes of our spirits all that exists in God's Kingdom and causes the realities of things to be made visible. By the help of this effulgent Light all the spiritual interpretation of the Holy Writings has been made plain, the hidden things of God's Universe have become manifest, and we have been enabled to comprehend the Divine purposes for man.

11 I pray that God in His mercy may illumine your hearts and souls with His glorious Light, then shall each one of you shine as a radiant star in the dark places of the world.

---

* Exodus 3:2.

23

SPIRITUAL ASPIRATION
IN THE WEST

'Abdu'l-Bahá said:

You are very welcome! From Eastern lands I have come to 1
the West to sojourn awhile among you. In the East it is often
said that the people of the West are without spirituality, but I
have not found it thus. Thank God, I see and feel that there
is much spiritual aspiration among the Western peoples, and
that in some cases their spiritual perception is even keener
than among their Eastern brothers. If the teaching given in
the East had been conscientiously spread in the West the
world today would be a more enlightened place.

Although in the past all the great Spiritual Teachers have 2
arisen in the East, there are still many men there who are
quite devoid of spirituality. With regard to the things of the
spirit they are as lifeless as a stone; nor do they wish to be
otherwise, for they consider that man is only a higher form
of animal and that the things of God concern him not.

But man's ambition should soar above this—he should 3
ever look higher than himself, ever upward and onward, until
through the Mercy of God he may come to the Kingdom
of Heaven. Again, there are men whose eyes are only open

to physical progress and to the evolution in the world of matter. These men prefer to study the resemblance between their own physical body and that of the ape, rather than to contemplate the glorious affiliation between their spirit and that of God. This is indeed strange, for it is only physically that man resembles the lower creation, with regard to his intellect he is totally unlike it.

4   Man is always progressing. His circle of knowledge is ever widening, and his mental activity flows through many and varied channels. Look what man has accomplished in the field of science, consider his many discoveries and countless inventions and his profound understanding of natural law.

5   In the world of art it is just the same, and this wonderful development of man's faculties becomes more and more rapid as time goes on. If the discoveries, inventions and material accomplishments of the last fifteen hundred years could be put together, you would see that there has been greater advancement during the last hundred years than in the previous fourteen centuries. For the rapidity with which man is progressing increases century by century.

6   The power of the intellect is one of God's greatest gifts to men, it is the power that makes him a higher creature than the animal. For whereas, century by century and age by age man's intelligence grows and becomes keener, that of the animal remains the same. They are no more intelligent today then they were a thousand years ago! Is there a greater proof than this needed to show man's dissimilarity to the animal creation? It is surely as clear as day.

7   As for the spiritual perfections they are man's birthright and belong to him alone of all creation. Man is, in reality, a spiritual being, and only when he lives in the spirit is he

truly happy. This spiritual longing and perception belongs to all men alike, and it is my firm conviction that the Western people possess great spiritual aspiration.

It is my fervent prayer that the star of the East will shed 8 its brilliant rays on the Western world, and that the people of the West may arise in strength, earnestness, and courage, to help their brethren in the East.

24

LECTURE GIVEN AT
A STUDIO IN PARIS

November 6th

This is in truth a Bahá'í house. Every time such a house or   1
meeting place is founded it becomes one of the greatest aids to
the general development of the town and country to which it
belongs. It encourages the growth of learning and science and
is known for its intense spirituality and for the love it spreads
among the peoples.

The foundation of such a meeting-place is always fol-   2
lowed by the greatest prosperity. The first Bahá'í Assembly
that existed in Ṭihrán was singularly blessed! In one year it
had grown so rapidly that its members had increased to nine
times their original number. Today, in far-away Persia, there
are many such assemblies where the friends of God meet
together in the fullness of joy, love and unity. They teach
the Cause of God, educate the ignorant, and draw heart to
heart in brotherly kindness. It is they who help the poor and
needy and give to them their daily bread. They love and care
for the sick and are messengers of hope and consolation to
the desolate and oppressed.

3   Oh, ye in Paris, strive that your assemblies may be like unto this, and may bear even greater fruits!

4   Oh, friends of God! If ye will trust in the Word of God and be strong; if ye will follow the precepts of Bahá'u'lláh to tend the sick, raise the fallen, care for the poor and needy, give shelter to the destitute, protect the oppressed, comfort the sorrowful and love the world of humanity with all your hearts, then I say unto you that erelong this meeting-place will see a wonderful harvest. Day by day each member will advance and become more and more spiritual. But ye must have a firm foundation and your aims and ambitions must be clearly understood by each member. They shall be as follows:

5   1. To show compassion and goodwill to all mankind.

6   2. To render service to humanity.

7   3. To endeavor to guide and enlighten those in darkness.

8   4. To be kind to everyone, and show forth affection to every living soul.

9   5. To be humble in your attitude towards God, to be constant in prayer to Him, so as to grow daily nearer to God.

10   6. To be so faithful and sincere in all your actions that every member may be known as embodying the qualities of honesty, love, faith, kindness, generosity, and courage. To be detached from all that is not God, attracted by the Heavenly Breath—a divine soul; so that the world may know that a Bahá'í is a perfect being.

11   Strive to attain this at these meetings. Then, indeed and in truth will ye, the friends of God, come together with great

joy! Render help one to the other, become as one man, having reached perfect unity.

I pray to God that daily ye may advance in spirituality, that God's love may be more and more manifested in you, that the thoughts of your hearts may be purified, and that your faces may be ever turned towards Him. May you one and all approach to the threshold of unity, and enter into the Kingdom. May each of you be like unto a flaming torch, lighted and burning bright with the fire of the Love of God. 12

25

BAHÁ'U'LLÁH

November 7th

'Abdu'l-Bahá said:

I will speak to you today of Bahá'u'lláh. In the third year 1
after the Báb had declared His Mission, Bahá'u'lláh, being
accused by fanatical Mullás of believing in the new doctrine,
was arrested and thrown into prison. The next day, however,
several ministers of the Government and other influential men
caused Him to be set free. Later on He was again arrested, and
the priests condemned Him to death! The Governor hesitated
to have this sentence carried out for fear of a revolution.
The priests met together in the Mosque, before which was
the place of execution. All the people of the town gathered
in crowds outside the Mosque. The carpenters brought their
saws and hammers, the butchers came with their knives, the
bricklayers and builders shouldered their spades, all these
men, incited by the frenzied Mullás, were eager to share in
the honor of killing Him. Inside the Mosque were assembled
the doctors of religion. Bahá'u'lláh stood before them, and
answered all their questions with great wisdom. The chief
sage in particular, was completely silenced by Bahá'u'lláh,
who refuted all his arguments.

2   A discussion arose between two of these priests as to the meaning of some words in the writings of the Báb; accusing Him of inaccuracy, they challenged Bahá'u'lláh to defend Him if He were able. These priests were entirely humiliated, for Bahá'u'lláh proved before the whole assembly that the Báb was absolutely right, and that the accusation was made in ignorance.

3   The defeated ones now put Him to the torture of the bastinado, and more infuriated than before brought Him out before the walls of the Mosque unto the place of execution, where the misguided people were awaiting His coming.

4   Still the Governor feared to comply with the demand of the priests for His execution. Realizing the danger in which the dignified prisoner was placed, some men were sent to rescue Him. In this they succeeded by breaking through the wall of the Mosque and leading Bahá'u'lláh through the opening into a place of safety, but not of freedom; for the Governor shifted the responsibility from off his own shoulders by sending Him to Ṭihrán. Here He was imprisoned in an underground dungeon, where the light of day was never seen. A heavy chain was placed about His neck by which He was chained to five other Bábís; these fetters were locked together by strong, very heavy bolts, and screws. His clothes were torn to pieces, also His fez. In this terrible condition He was kept for four months.

5   During this time none of His friends were able to get access to Him.

6   A prison official made an attempt to poison Him but, beyond causing Him great suffering, this poison had no effect.

7   After a time the Government liberated Him and exiled Him and His family to Baghdád, where He remained for eleven

years. During this time He underwent severe persecutions, being surrounded by the watchful hatred of His enemies.

He bore all evils and torments with the greatest courage and fortitude. Often when He arose in the morning, He knew not whether He would live until the sun should set. Meanwhile, each day, the priests came and questioned Him on religion and metaphysics.

At length the Turkish Governor exiled Him to Constantinople, whence He was sent to Adrianople; here He stayed for five years. Eventually, He was sent to the far off prison fortress of St. Jean d'Acre. Here He was imprisoned in the military portion of the fortress and kept under the strictest surveillance. Words would fail me to tell you of the many trials He had to suffer, and all the misery He endured in that prison. Notwithstanding, it was from this prison that Bahá'u'lláh wrote to all the Monarchs of Europe, and these letters with one exception were sent through the post.

The Epistle of Náṣiri'd-Dín Sháh was confided to a Persian Bahá'í, Mírzá Badí' Khurásání, who undertook to deliver it into the Sháh's own hands. This brave man waited in the neighborhood of Ṭihrán for the passing of the Sháh, who had the intention to journey by that way to his Summer Palace. The courageous messenger followed the Sháh to his Palace, and waited on the road near the entrance for several days. Always in the same place was he seen waiting on the road, until the people began to wonder why he should be there. At last the Sháh heard of him, and commanded his servants that the man should be brought before him.

"Oh! servants of the Sháh, I bring a letter, which I must deliver into his own hands," Badí' said, and then Badí' said to the Sháh, "I bring you a letter from Bahá'u'lláh!"

12   He was immediately seized and questioned by those who wished to elicit information which would help them in the further persecutions of Bahá'u'lláh. Badí' would not answer a word; then they tortured him, still he held his peace! After three days they killed him, having failed to force him to speak! These cruel men photographed him whilst he was under torture.*

13   The Sháh gave the letter from Bahá'u'lláh to the priests that they might explain it to him. After some days these priests told the Sháh that the letter was from a political enemy. The Sháh grew angry and said, "This is no explanation. I pay you to read and answer my letters, therefore obey!"

14   The spirit and meaning of the Tablet to Náṣiri'd-Dín Sháh was, in short, this: "Now that the time has come, when the Cause of the Glory of God has appeared, I ask that I may be allowed to come to Ṭihrán and answer any questions the priests may put to Me.

15   "I exhort you to detach yourself from the worldly magnificence of your Empire. Remember all those great kings who have lived before you—their glories have passed away!"

16   The letter was written in a most beautiful manner, and continued warning the King and telling him of the future triumph of the Kingdom of Bahá'u'lláh, both in the Eastern and in the Western World.

17   The Sháh paid no attention to the warning of this letter and continued to live in the same fashion until the end.

---

* A certain man who was present when Badí' was told he should carry the Epistle to the Sháh saw him transfigured; he became radiant.

Although Bahá'u'lláh was in prison the great Power of the   18
Holy Spirit was with Him!

None other in prison could have been like unto Him. In   19
spite of all the hardships He suffered, He never complained.

In the dignity of His Majesty, He always refused to see the   20
Governor, or the influential people of the town.

Although the surveillance was unremittingly strict He came   21
and went as He wished! He died in a house situated about
three kilometers from St. Jean d'Acre.

26

GOOD IDEAS MUST BE CARRIED INTO ACTION

November 8th

All over the world one hears beautiful sayings extolled and   1
noble precepts admired. All men say they love what is good,
and hate everything that is evil! Sincerity is to be admired,
whilst lying is despicable. Faith is a virtue, and treachery is
a disgrace to humanity. It is a blessed thing to gladden the
hearts of men, and wrong to be the cause of pain. To be kind
and merciful is right, while to hate is sinful. Justice is a noble
quality and injustice an iniquity. That it is one's duty to be
pitiful and harm no one, and to avoid jealousy and malice at
all costs. Wisdom is the glory of man, not ignorance; light,
not darkness! It is a good thing to turn one's face toward God,
and foolishness to ignore Him. That it is our duty to guide
man upward, and not to mislead him and be the cause of
his downfall. There are many more examples like unto these.

But all these sayings are but words and we see very few of
them carried into the world of action. On the contrary, we   2
perceive that men are carried away by passion and selfishness,
each man thinking only of what will benefit himself even if it
means the ruin of his brother. They are all anxious to make

their fortune and care little or nothing for the welfare of others. They are concerned about their *own* peace and comfort, while the condition of their fellows troubles them not at all.

3   Unhappily this is the road most men tread.

4   But Bahá'ís must not be thus; they must rise above this condition. Actions must be more to them than words. By their actions they must be merciful and not merely by their words. They must on all occasions confirm by their actions what they proclaim in words. Their deeds must prove their fidelity, and their actions must show forth Divine light.

5   Let your actions cry aloud to the world that you are indeed Bahá'ís, for it is *actions* that speak to the world and are the cause of the progress of humanity.

6   If we are true Bahá'ís speech is not needed. Our actions will help on the world, will spread civilization, will help the progress of science, and cause the arts to develop. Without action nothing in the material world can be accomplished, neither can words unaided advance a man in the spiritual Kingdom. It is not through lip-service only that the elect of God have attained to holiness, but by patient lives of active service they have brought light into the world.

7   Therefore strive that your actions day by day may be beautiful prayers. Turn towards God, and seek always to do that which is right and noble. Enrich the poor, raise the fallen, comfort the sorrowful, bring healing to the sick, reassure the fearful, rescue the oppressed, bring hope to the hopeless, shelter the destitute!

8   This is the work of a true Bahá'í, and this is what is expected of him. If we strive to do all this, then are we true Bahá'ís, but if we neglect it, we are not followers of the Light, and we have no right to the name.

God, who sees all hearts, knows how far our lives are the   9
fulfillment of our words.

27

THE TRUE MEANING OF BAPTISM BY WATER AND FIRE

November 9th

In the Gospel according to St. John, Christ has said: "Except 1 a man be born of water and the Spirit, he cannot enter into the Kingdom of Heaven."* The priests have interpreted this into meaning that baptism is necessary for salvation. In another Gospel it is said: "He shall baptize you with the Holy Ghost and with fire."†

Thus the water of baptism and the fire are one! It cannot 2 mean that the "water" spoken of is *physical* water, for it is the direct opposite of "fire," and one destroys the other. When in the Gospels, Christ speaks of "water," He means *that which causes life,* for without water no worldly creature can live—mineral, vegetable, animal and man, one and all, depend upon water for their very being. Yes, the latest scientific

---

* John 3:5.
† Matthew 3:11.

97

discoveries prove to us that even mineral has some form of life, and that it also needs water for its existence.

3   Water is the cause of life, and when Christ speaks of water, He is symbolizing that which is the cause of *Everlasting Life.*

4   This life-giving water of which He speaks is like unto fire, for it is none other than the Love of God, and this love means life to our souls.

5   By the fire of the Love of God the veil is burnt which separates us from the Heavenly Realities, and with clear vision we are enabled to struggle onward and upward, ever progressing in the paths of virtue and holiness, and becoming the means of light to the world.

6   There is nothing greater or more blessed than the Love of God! It gives healing to the sick, balm to the wounded, joy and consolation to the whole world, and through it alone can man attain Life Everlasting. The *essence* of all religions is the Love of God, and it is the foundation of all the sacred teachings.

7   It was the Love of God that led Abraham, Isaac, and Jacob, that strengthened Joseph in Egypt and gave to Moses courage and patience.

8   Through the Love of God, Christ was sent into the world with His inspiring example of a perfect life of self-sacrifice and devotion, bringing to men the message of Eternal Life. It was the Love of God that gave Muḥammad power to bring the Arabs from a state of animal degradation to a loftier state of existence.

9   God's Love it was that sustained the Báb and brought Him to His supreme sacrifice, and made His bosom the willing target for a thousand bullets.

Finally, it was the Love of God that gave to the East 10
Bahá'u'lláh, and is now sending the light of His teaching far
into the West, and from Pole to Pole.

Thus I exhort each of you, realizing its power and beauty, 11
to sacrifice all your thoughts, words and actions to bring the
knowledge of the Love of God into every heart.

28

DISCOURSE AT "L'ALLIANCE SPIRITUALISTE"

Salle de l'Athénée,
St. Germain, Paris,
November 9th

I wish to express my gratitude for your hospitality, and my   1
joy that you are spiritually minded. I am happy to be present
at a gathering such as this, assembled together to listen to a
Divine Message. If you could see with the eye of truth, great
waves of spirituality would be visible to you in this place. The
power of the Holy Spirit is here for all. Praise be to God that
your hearts are inspired with Divine fervor! Your souls are as
waves on the sea of the spirit; although each individual is a
distinct wave, the ocean is one, all are united in God.

Every heart should radiate unity, so that the Light of the   2
one Divine Source of all may shine forth bright and luminous. We must not consider the separate waves alone, but the
entire sea. We should rise from the individual to the whole.
The spirit is as one great ocean and the waves thereof are the
souls of men.

3   We are told in the Holy Scripture that the New Jerusalem shall appear on earth. Now it is evident that this celestial city is not built of material stones and mortar, but that it is a city not made with hands, eternal in the Heavens.

4   This is a prophetic symbol, meaning the coming again of the Divine Teaching to enlighten the hearts of men. It is long since this Holy Guidance has governed the lives of humanity. But now, at last, the Holy City of the New Jerusalem has come again to the world, it has appeared anew under an Eastern sky; from the horizon of Persia has its effulgence arisen to be a light to lighten the whole world. We see in these days the fulfillment of the Divine Prophecy. Jerusalem had disappeared. The heavenly city was destroyed, now it is rebuilt; it was razed to the ground, but now its walls and pinnacles have been restored, and are towering aloft in their renewed and glorious beauty.

5   In the Western world material prosperity has triumphed, whilst in the East the spiritual sun has shone forth. I am very glad to see such an assembly as this in Paris, where spiritual and material progress are met together in unity.

6   Man—the true man—is soul, not body; though physically man belongs to the animal kingdom, yet his soul lifts him above the rest of creation. Behold how the light of the sun illuminates the world of matter: even so doth the Divine Light shed its rays in the kingdom of the soul. The soul it is which makes the human creature a celestial entity!

7   By the power of the Holy Spirit, working through his soul, man is able to perceive the Divine reality of things. All great works of art and science are witnesses to this power of the Spirit.

8   The same Spirit gives Eternal Life.

Those alone who are baptized by the Divine Spirit will be   9
enabled to bring all peoples into the bond of unity. It is by
the power of the Spirit that the Eastern World of spiritual
thought can intermingle with the Western realm of action,
so that the world of matter may become Divine.

It follows that all who work for the Supreme Design are   10
soldiers in the army of the Spirit.

The light of the celestial world makes war against the world   11
of shadow and illusion. The rays of the Sun of Truth dispel
the darkness of superstition and misunderstanding.

You are of the Spirit! To you who seek the truth, the Revela-   12
tion of Bahá'u'lláh will come as a great joy! This teaching is of
the Spirit, in it is no precept which is not of the Divine Spirit.

Spirit cannot be perceived by the material senses of the   13
physical body, excepting as it is expressed in outward signs
and works. The human body is visible, the soul is invisible.
It is the soul nevertheless that directs a man's faculties, that
governs his humanity.

The soul has two main faculties. (a) As outer circumstances   14
are communicated to the soul by the eyes, ears, and brain of
a man, so does the soul communicate its desires and purposes
through the brain to the hands and tongue of the physical
body, thereby expressing itself. The spirit in the soul is the
very essence of life. (b) The second faculty of the soul expresses itself in the world of vision, where the soul inhabited
by the spirit has its being, and functions without the help of
the material bodily senses. There, in the realm of vision, the
soul sees without the help of the physical eye, hears without
the aid of the physical ear, and travels without dependence
upon physical motion. It is, therefore, clear that the spirit in
the soul of man can function through the physical body by

using the organs of the ordinary senses, and that it is able also to live and act without their aid in the world of vision. This proves without a doubt the superiority of the soul of man over his body, the superiority of spirit over matter.

15   For example, look at this lamp: is not the light within it superior to the lamp which holds it? However beautiful the form of the lamp may be, if the light is not there its purpose is unfulfilled, it is without life—a dead thing. The lamp needs the light, but the light does not need the lamp.

16   The spirit does not need a body, but the body needs spirit, or it cannot live. The soul can live without a body, but the body without a soul dies.

17   If a man lose his sight, his hearing, his hand or his foot, should his soul still inhabit the body he lives, and is able to manifest divine virtues. On the other hand, without the spirit it would be impossible for a perfect body to exist.

18   The greatest power of the Holy Spirit exists in the Divine Manifestations of the Truth. Through the power of the Spirit the Heavenly Teaching has been brought into the World of Humanity. Through the power of the Spirit life everlasting has come to the children of men. Through the power of the Spirit the Divine Glory has shone from East to West, and through the power of the same Spirit will the divine virtues of humanity become manifest.

19   Our greatest efforts must be directed towards detachment from the things of the world; we must strive to become more spiritual, more luminous, to follow the counsel of the Divine Teaching, to serve the cause of unity and true equality, to be merciful, to reflect the love of the Highest on all men, so that the light of the Spirit shall be apparent in all our deeds, to the end that all humanity shall be united, the stormy sea

thereof calmed, and all rough waves disappear from off the surface of life's ocean henceforth unruffled and peaceful. Then will the New Jerusalem be seen by mankind, who will enter through its gates and receive the Divine Bounty.

I thank God that I have been present amongst you this afternoon, and I thank you for your spiritual feeling. 20

I pray that you may grow in Divine fervor, and that the power of unity in the Spirit will augment, so that the prophecies may be fulfilled, and that in this great century of the Light of God all the glad tidings written in the Sacred Books may come to pass. This is the glorious time of which the Lord Jesus Christ spoke when He told us to pray "Thy Kingdom come, Thy Will be done on earth as it is in Heaven." I hope that this is also your expectation and great desire. 21

We are united in the one aim and hope that all shall be as one and every heart illumined by the Love of our Divine Father, God! 22

May all our actions be spiritual, and all our interests and affections be centered in the Kingdom of Glory! 23

29

THE EVOLUTION
OF THE SPIRIT

15 Rue Greuze, Paris,
November 10th

'Abdu'l-Bahá said:

Tonight I will speak of the evolution or progress of the   1
spirit.

Absolute repose does not exist in nature. All things either   2
make progress or lose ground. Everything moves forward or
backward, nothing is without motion. From his birth, a man
progresses physically until he reaches maturity, then, having
arrived at the prime of his life, he begins to decline, the strength
and powers of his body decrease, and he gradually arrives at
the hour of death. Likewise a plant progresses from the seed to
maturity, then its life begins to lessen until it fades and dies. A
bird soars to a certain height and having reached the highest
possible point in its flight, begins its descent to earth.

Thus it is evident that movement is essential to all exis-   3
tence. All material things progress to a certain point, then
begin to decline. This is the law which governs the whole
physical creation.

4   Now let us consider the soul. We have seen that movement is essential to existence; nothing that has life is without motion. All creation, whether of the mineral, vegetable or animal kingdom, is compelled to obey the law of motion; it must either ascend or descend. But with the human soul, there is no decline. Its only movement is towards perfection; growth and progress alone constitute the motion of the soul.

5   Divine perfection is infinite, therefore the progress of the soul is also infinite. From the very birth of a human being the soul progresses, the intellect grows and knowledge increases. When the body dies the soul lives on. All the differing degrees of created physical beings are limited, but the soul is limitless!

6   In all religions the belief exists that the soul survives the death of the body. Intercessions are sent up for the beloved dead, prayers are said for their progress and for the forgiveness of their sins. If the soul perished with the body all this would have no meaning. Further, if it were not possible for the soul to advance towards perfection after it had been released from the body, of what avail are all these loving prayers, of devotion?

7   We read in the sacred writings that "all good works are found again."* Now, if the soul did not survive, this also would mean nothing!

8   The very fact that our spiritual instinct, surely never given in vain, prompts us to pray for the welfare of those, our loved ones, who have passed out of the material world: does it not bear witness to the continuance of their existence?

---

* i.e.—All good actions bring their own reward.

In the world of spirit there is no retrogression. The world   9
of mortality is a world of contradictions, of opposites; motion being compulsory everything must either go forward or
retreat. In the realm of spirit there is no retreat possible, all
movement is bound to be towards a perfect state. "Progress"
is the expression of spirit in the world of matter. The intelligence of man, his reasoning powers, his knowledge, his
scientific achievements, all these being manifestations of the
spirit, partake of the inevitable law of spiritual progress and
are, therefore, of necessity, immortal.

My hope for you is that you will progress in the world of   10
spirit, as well as in the world of matter; that your intelligence
will develop, your knowledge will augment, and your understanding be widened.

You must ever press forward, never standing still; avoid   11
stagnation, the first step to a backward movement, to decay.

The whole physical creation is perishable. These material   12
bodies are composed of atoms; when these atoms begin to
separate decomposition sets in, then comes what we call
death. This composition of atoms, which constitutes the body
or mortal element of any created being, is temporary. When
the power of attraction, which holds these atoms together,
is withdrawn, the body, as such, ceases to exist.

With the soul it is different. The soul is not a combination   13
of elements, it is not composed of many atoms, it is of one
indivisible substance and therefore eternal. It is entirely out
of the order of the physical creation; it is immortal!

Scientific philosophy has demonstrated that a *simple* ele-   14
ment ("simple" meaning "not composed") is indestructible,
eternal. The soul, not being a composition of elements, is,

in character, as a simple element, and therefore cannot cease to exist.

15   The soul, being of that one indivisible substance, can suffer neither disintegration nor destruction, therefore there is no reason for its coming to an end. All things living show signs of their existence, and it follows that these signs could not of themselves exist if that which they express or to which they testify had no being. A thing which does not exist, can, of course, give no sign of its existence. The manifold signs of the existence of the spirit are forever before us.

16   The traces of the Spirit of Jesus Christ, the influence of His Divine Teaching, are present with us today, and are everlasting.

17   A nonexistent thing, it is agreed, cannot be seen by signs. In order to write a man must exist—one who does not exist cannot write. Writing is, in itself, a sign of the writer's soul and intelligence. The Sacred Writings (with ever the same Teaching) prove the continuity of the spirit.

18   Consider the aim of creation: is it possible that all is created to evolve and develop through countless ages with this small goal in view—a few years of a man's life on earth? Is it not unthinkable that this should be the final aim of existence?

19   The mineral evolves till it is absorbed in the life of the plant, the plant progresses till finally it loses its life in that of the animal; the animal, in its turn, forming part of the food of man, is absorbed into human life.

20   Thus, man is shown to be the sum of all creation, the superior of all created beings, the goal to which countless ages of existence have progressed.

21   At the best, man spends four-score years and ten in this world—a short time indeed!

Does a man cease to exist when he leaves the body? If his 22 life comes to an end, then all the previous evolution is useless, all has been for nothing! Can one imagine that Creation has no greater aim than this?

The soul is eternal, immortal. 23

Materialists say, "Where is the soul? What is it? We cannot 24 see it, neither can we touch it."

This is how we must answer them: However much the 25 mineral may progress, it cannot comprehend the vegetable world. Now, that lack of comprehension does not prove the nonexistence of the plant!

To however great a degree the plant may have evolved, it 26 is unable to understand the animal world; this ignorance is no proof that the animal does not exist!

The animal, be he never so highly developed, cannot 27 imagine the intelligence of man, neither can he realize the nature of his soul. But, again, this does not prove that man is without intellect, or without soul. It only demonstrates this, that one form of existence is incapable of comprehending a form superior to itself.

This flower may be unconscious of such a being as man, 28 but the fact of its ignorance does not prevent the existence of humanity.

In the same way, if materialists do not believe in the existence 29 of the soul, their unbelief does not prove that there is no such realm as the world of spirit. The very existence of man's intelligence proves his immortality; moreover, darkness proves the presence of light, for without light there would be no shadow. Poverty proves the existence of riches, for, without riches, how could we measure poverty? Ignorance proves that knowledge exists, for without knowledge how could there be ignorance?

30   Therefore the idea of mortality presupposes the existence of immortality—for if there were no Life Eternal, there would be no way of measuring the life of this world!

31   If the spirit were not immortal, how could the Manifestations of God endure such terrible trials?

32   Why did Christ Jesus suffer the fearful death on the cross?

33   Why did Muḥammad bear persecutions?

34   Why did the Báb make the supreme sacrifice and why did Bahá'u'lláh pass the years of His life in prison?

35   Why should all this suffering have been, if not to prove the everlasting life of the spirit?

36   Christ suffered, He accepted all His trials because of the immortality of His spirit. If a man reflects he will understand the spiritual significance of the law of progress; how all moves from the inferior to the superior degree.

37   It is only a man without intelligence who, after considering these things, can imagine that the great scheme of creation should suddenly cease to progress, that evolution should come to such an inadequate end!

38   Materialists who reason in this way, and contend that we are unable to *see* the world of spirit, or to perceive the blessings of God, are surely like the animals who have no understanding; having eyes they see not, ears they have, but do not hear. And this lack of sight and hearing is a proof of nothing but their own inferiority; of whom we read in the Qur'án, "They are men who are blind and deaf to the Spirit." They do not use that great gift of God, the power of the understanding, by which they might see with the eyes of the spirit, hear with spiritual ears and also comprehend with a Divinely enlightened heart.

The inability of the materialistic mind to grasp the idea of   39
the Life Eternal is no proof of the nonexistence of that life.

The comprehension of that other life depends on our   40
spiritual birth!

My prayer for you is that your spiritual faculties and as-   41
pirations may daily increase, and that you will never allow
the material senses to veil from your eyes the glories of the
Heavenly Illumination.

30

THE DESIRES AND PRAYERS OF 'ABDU'L-BAHÁ

November 15th

'Abdu'l-Bahá said:

You are all very welcome, and I love you all most dearly. 1

Day and night I pray to Heaven for you that strength may 2
be yours, and that, one and all, you may participate in the
blessings of Bahá'u'lláh, and enter into the Kingdom.

I supplicate that you may become as new beings, illumined 3
with the Divine Light, like unto shining lamps, and that from
one end of Europe to the other the knowledge of the Love
of God may spread.

May this boundless love so fill your hearts and minds that 4
sadness may find no room to enter and may you with joyful
hearts soar like birds into the Divine Radiance.

May your hearts become clear and pure like unto polished 5
mirrors in which may be reflected the full glory of the Sun
of Truth.

May your eyes be opened to see the signs of the Kingdom 6
of God, and may your ears be unstopped so that you may

hear with a perfect understanding the Heavenly Proclamation sounding in your midst.

7   May your souls receive help and comfort, and, being so strengthened, may they be enabled to live in accordance with the teachings of Bahá'u'lláh.

8   I pray for each and all that you may be as flames of love in the world, and that the brightness of your light and the warmth of your affection may reach the heart of every sad and sorrowing child of God.

9   May you be as shining stars, bright and luminous forever in the Kingdom.

10   I counsel you that you study earnestly the teachings of Bahá'u'lláh, so that, God helping you, you may in deed and truth become Bahá'ís.

31

CONCERNING BODY, SOUL AND SPIRIT

4 Avenue de Camoëns, Paris,
Friday morning, November 17th

There are in the world of humanity three degrees; those of the body, the soul, and spirit. 1

The body is the physical or animal degree of man. From the bodily point of view man is a sharer of the animal kingdom. The bodies alike of men and animals are composed of elements held together by the law of attraction. 2

Like the animal, man possesses the faculties of the senses, is subject to heat, cold, hunger, thirst, etc.; unlike the animal, man has a rational soul, the human intelligence. 3

This intelligence of man is the intermediary between his body and his spirit. 4

When man allows the spirit, through his soul, to enlighten his understanding, then does he contain all Creation; because man, being the culmination of all that went before and thus superior to all previous evolutions, contains all the lower world within himself. Illumined by the spirit through the instrumentality of the soul, man's radiant intelligence makes him the crowning-point of Creation. 5

6   But on the other hand, when man does not open his mind
and heart to the blessing of the spirit, but turns his soul towards the material side, towards the bodily part of his nature,
then is he fallen from his high place and he becomes inferior
to the inhabitants of the lower animal kingdom. In this case
the man is in a sorry plight! For if the spiritual qualities of
the soul, open to the breath of the Divine Spirit, are never
used, they become atrophied, enfeebled, and at last incapable;
whilst the soul's material qualities alone being exercised, they
become terribly powerful—and the unhappy, misguided
man, becomes more savage, more unjust, more vile, more
cruel, more malevolent than the lower animals themselves.
All his aspirations and desires being strengthened by the
lower side of the soul's nature, he becomes more and more
brutal, until his whole being is in no way superior to that of
the beasts that perish. Men such as this plan to work evil, to
hurt and to destroy; they are entirely without the spirit of
Divine compassion, for the celestial quality of the soul has
been dominated by that of the material. If, on the contrary,
the spiritual nature of the soul has been so strengthened that
it holds the material side in subjection, then does the man
approach the Divine; his humanity becomes so glorified that
the virtues of the Celestial Assembly are manifested in him;
he radiates the Mercy of God, he stimulates the spiritual
progress of mankind, for he becomes a lamp to show light
on their path.

7   You perceive how the soul is the intermediary between the
body and the spirit. In like manner is this tree* the intermediary between the seed and the fruit. When the fruit of the

---

* A small orange-tree on the table nearby.

tree appears and becomes ripe, then we know that the tree is perfect; if the tree bore no fruit it would be merely a useless growth, serving no purpose!

When a soul has in it the life of the spirit, then does it   8
bring forth good fruit and become a Divine tree. I wish you to try to understand this example. I hope that the unspeakable goodness of God will so strengthen you that the celestial quality of your soul, which relates it to the spirit, will forever dominate the material side, so entirely ruling the senses that your soul will approach the perfections of the Heavenly Kingdom. May your faces, being steadfastly set towards the Divine Light, become so luminous that all your thoughts, words and actions will shine with the Spiritual Radiance dominating your souls, so that in the gatherings of the world you will show perfection in your life.

Some men's lives are solely occupied with the things of   9
this world; their minds are so circumscribed by exterior manners and traditional interests that they are blind to any other realm of existence, to the spiritual significance of all things! They think and dream of earthly fame, of material progress. Sensuous delights and comfortable surroundings bound their horizon, their highest ambitions center in successes of worldly conditions and circumstances! They curb not their lower propensities; they eat, drink, and sleep! Like the animal, they have no thought beyond their own physical well-being. It is true that these necessities must be dispatched. Life is a load which must be carried on while we are on earth, but the cares of the lower things of life should not be allowed to monopolize all the thoughts and aspirations of a human being. The heart's ambitions should ascend to a more glorious goal, mental activity should rise to higher levels! Men should

hold in their souls the vision of celestial perfection, and there prepare a dwelling-place for the inexhaustible bounty of the Divine Spirit.

10   Let your ambition be the achievement on earth of a Heavenly civilization! I ask for you the supreme blessing, that you may be so filled with the vitality of the Heavenly Spirit that you may be the cause of life to the world.

32

THE BAHÁ'ÍS MUST WORK WITH HEART AND SOUL TO BRING ABOUT A BETTER CONDITION IN THE WORLD

November 19th

How joyful it is to see such a meeting as this, for it is in truth a gathering together of "heavenly men." 1

We are all united in one Divine purpose, no material motive is ours, and our dearest wish is to spread the Love of God throughout the world! 2

We work and pray for the unity of mankind, that all the races of the earth may become one race, all the countries one country, and that all hearts may beat as one heart, working together for perfect unity and brotherhood. 3

Praise be to God that our efforts are sincere and that our hearts are turned to the Kingdom. Our greatest longing is that truth may be established in the world, and in this hope we draw near to one another in love and affection. Each and all are wholehearted and selfless, willing to sacrifice all personal ambition to the grand ideal towards which they strive: Brotherly love and peace and union among men! 4

5   Doubt not that God is with us, on our right hand and on our left, that day by day He will cause our numbers to increase, and that our meetings will grow in strength and usefulness.

6   It is my dearest hope that you may all become a blessing to others, that you may give sight to the spiritually blind, hearing to the spiritually deaf and life to those who are dead in sin.

7   May you help those sunk in materiality to realize their Divine son-ship, and encourage them to arise and be worthy of their birthright; so that by your endeavor the world of humanity may become the Kingdom of God and of His elect.

8   I thank God that we are at one in this grand ideal, that my longings are also yours and that we work together in perfect unity.

9   Today, upon the earth, one sees the sad spectacle of cruel war! Man slays his brother man for selfish gain, and to enlarge his territories! For this ignoble ambition hate has taken possession of his heart, and more and more blood is shed!

10   Fresh battles are fought, the armies are increased, more cannon, more guns, more explosives of all kinds are sent out—so does bitterness and hate augment from day to day!

11   But this assembly, thank God, longs only for peace and unity, and must work with heart and soul to bring about a better condition in the world.

12   You who are the servants of God fight against oppression, hate and discord, so that wars may cease and God's laws of peace and love may be established among men.

13   Work! Work with all your strength, spread the Cause of the Kingdom among men; teach the self-sufficient to turn humbly towards God, the sinful to sin no more, and await with glad expectation the coming of the Kingdom.

Love and obey your Heavenly Father, and rest assured 14
that Divine help is yours. Verily I say unto you that you shall
indeed conquer the world!

Only have faith, patience and courage—this is but the 15
beginning, but surely you will succeed, for God is with you!

33

ON CALUMNY

Monday, November 20th

From the beginning of the world until the present time each   1
"Manifestation"* sent from God has been opposed by an
embodiment of the "Powers of Darkness."

This dark power has always endeavored to extinguish the   2
light. Tyranny has ever sought to overcome justice. Ignorance
has persistently tried to trample knowledge underfoot. This
has, from the earliest ages, been the method of the material
world.

In the time of Moses, Pharaoh set himself to prevent the   3
Mosaic Light being spread abroad.

In the day of Christ, Annas and Caiaphas inflamed the   4
Jewish people against Him and the learned doctors of Israel
joined together to resist His Power. All sorts of calumnies were
circulated against Him. The Scribes and Pharisees conspired
to make the people believe Him to be a liar, an apostate, and
a blasphemer. They spread these slanders throughout the

---

* i.e.—Divine Manifestation.

whole Eastern world against Christ, and caused Him to be condemned to a shameful death!

5   In the case of Muḥammad also, the learned doctors of His day determined to extinguish the light of His influence. They tried by the power of the sword to prevent the spread of His teaching.

6   In spite of all their efforts the Sun of Truth shone forth from the horizon. In every case the army of light vanquished the powers of darkness on the battlefield of the world, and the radiance of the Divine Teaching illumined the earth. Those who accepted the Teaching and worked for the Cause of God became luminous stars in the sky of humanity.

7   Now, in our own day, history repeats itself.

8   Those who would have men believe that religion is their own private property once more bring their efforts to bear against the Sun of Truth: they resist the Command of God; they invent calumnies, not having arguments against it, neither proofs. They attack with masked faces, not daring to come forth into the light of day.

9   Our methods are different, we do not attack, neither calumniate; we do not wish to dispute with them; we bring forth proofs and arguments; we invite them to confute our statements. They cannot answer us, but instead, they write all they can think of against the Divine Messenger, Bahá'u'lláh.

10   Do not let your hearts be troubled by these defamatory writings! Obey the words of Bahá'u'lláh and answer them not. Rejoice, rather, that even these falsehoods will result in the spread of the truth. When these slanders appear inquiries are made, and those who inquire are led into a knowledge of the Faith.

If a man were to declare, "There is a lamp in the next room   11
which gives no light," one hearer might be satisfied with his
report, but a wiser man goes into the room to judge for himself, and behold, when he finds the light shining brilliantly
in the lamp, he knows the truth!

Again, a man proclaims: "There lies a garden in which there   12
are trees with broken branches bearing no fruit, and the leaves
thereof are faded and yellow! In that garden, also, there are
flowering plants with no blooms, and rose bushes withered
and dying—go not into that garden!" A just man, hearing this
account of the garden, would not be content without seeing
for himself whether it be true or not. He, therefore, enters
the garden, and behold, he finds it well tilled; the branches
of the trees are sturdy and strong, being also loaded with the
sweetest of ripe fruits amongst the luxuriance of beautiful
green leaves. The flowering plants are bright with many-hued
blossoms; the rose bushes are covered with fragrant and lovely
roses and all is verdant and well tended. When the glory of
the garden is spread out before the eyes of the just man, he
praises God that, through unworthy calumny, he has been
led into a place of such wondrous beauty!

This is the result of the slanderer's work: to be the cause   13
of guiding men to a discovery of the truth.

We know that all the falsehoods spread about Christ and   14
His apostles and all the books written against Him, only led
the people to inquire into His doctrine; then, having seen
the beauty and inhaled the fragrance, they walked evermore
amidst the roses and the fruits of that celestial garden.

Therefore, I say unto you, spread the Divine Truth with all   15
your might that men's intelligence may become enlightened;

this is the best answer to those who slander. I do not wish to speak of those people nor to say anything ill of them—only to tell you that slander is of no importance!

16 Clouds may veil the sun, but, be they never so dense, his rays will penetrate! Nothing can prevent the radiance of the sun descending to warm and vivify the Divine Garden.

17 Nothing can prevent the fall of the rain from Heaven.

18 Nothing can prevent the fulfillment of the Word of God!

19 Therefore when you see books and papers written against the Revelation, be not distressed, but take comfort in the assurance that the cause will thereby gain strength.

20 No one casts stones at a tree without fruit. No one tries to extinguish a lamp without light!

21 Regard the former times. Had the calumnies of Pharaoh any effect? He affirmed that Moses was a murderer, that he had slain a man and deserved to be executed! He also declared that Moses and Aaron were fomenters of discord, that they tried to destroy the religion of Egypt and therefore must be put to death. These words of Pharaoh were vainly spoken. The light of Moses shone. The radiance of the Law of God has encircled the world!

22 When the Pharisees said of Christ that He had broken the Sabbath Day, that He had defied the Law of Moses, that He had threatened to destroy the Temple and the Holy City of Jerusalem, and that He deserved to be crucified—We know that all these slanderous attacks had no result in hindering the spread of the Gospel!

23 The Sun of Christ shone brilliantly in the sky, and the breath of the Holy Spirit wafted over the whole earth!

24 And I say unto you that no calumny is able to prevail against the Light of God; it can only result in causing it to be

more universally recognized. If a cause were of no significance, who would take the trouble to work against it!

But always the greater the cause the more do enemies arise   25
in larger and larger numbers to attempt its overthrow! The brighter the light the darker the shadow! Our part it is to act in accordance with the teaching of Bahá'u'lláh in humility and firm steadfastness.

34

THERE CAN BE NO TRUE HAPPINESS AND PROGRESS WITHOUT SPIRITUALITY

November 21st

Ferocity and savagery are natural to animals, but men should   1
show forth the qualities of love and affection. God sent all His
Prophets into the world with one aim, to sow in the hearts of
men love and goodwill, and for this great purpose they were
willing to suffer and to die. All the sacred Books were written
to lead and direct man into the ways of love and unity; and
yet, in spite of all this, we have the sad spectacle of war and
bloodshed in our midst.

When we look into the pages of history, past and present,   2
we see the black earth reddened by human blood. Men kill
each other like the savage wolves, and forget the laws of love
and tolerance.

Now this luminous age has come, bringing with it won-   3
derful civilization and material progress. Men's intellects
have widened, their perceptions grown, but alas, in spite
of all this, fresh blood is being spilt day by day. Look at the
present Turco-Italian war; consider for a moment the fate of
these unhappy people! How many have been killed during

this sad time? How many homes are ruined, wives desolate, and children orphans! And what is to be gained in exchange for all this anguish and heartache? Only a corner of the earth!

4   This all shows that material progress alone does not tend to uplift man. On the contrary, the more he becomes immersed in material progress, the more does his spirituality become obscured.

5   In times gone by progress on the material plane was not so rapid, neither was there bloodshed in such profusion. In ancient warfare there were no cannons, no guns, no dynamite, no shells, no torpedo boats, no battleships, no submarines. Now, owing to material civilization, we have all these inventions, and war goes from bad to worse! Europe itself has become like one immense arsenal, full of explosives, and may God prevent its ignition—for, should this happen, the whole world would be involved.

6   I want to make you understand that *material* progress and spiritual progress are two very different things, and that only if material progress goes hand in hand with spirituality can any real progress come about, and the Most Great Peace reign in the world. If men followed the Holy Counsels and the Teachings of the Prophets, if Divine Light shone in all hearts and men were really religious, we should soon see peace on earth and the Kingdom of God among men. The laws of God may be likened unto the soul and material progress unto the body. If the body were not animated by the soul, it would cease to exist. It is my earnest prayer that spirituality may ever grow and increase in the world, so that customs may become enlightened and peace and concord may be established.

7   War and rapine with their attendant cruelties are an abomination to God, and bring their own punishment, for the God

of love is also a God of justice and each man must inevitably reap what he sows. Let us try to understand the commands of the Most High and to order our lives as He directs. True happiness depends on spiritual good and having the heart ever open to receive the Divine Bounty.

If the heart turns away from the blessings God offers how   8 can it hope for happiness? If it does not put its hope and trust in God's Mercy, where can it find rest? Oh, trust in God! for His Bounty is everlasting, and in His Blessings, for they are superb. Oh! put your faith in the Almighty, for He faileth not and His goodness endureth forever! His Sun giveth Light continually, and the Clouds of His Mercy are full of the Waters of Compassion with which He waters the hearts of all who trust in Him. His refreshing Breeze ever carries healing in its wings to the parched souls of men! Is it wise to turn away from such a loving Father, Who showers His blessings upon us, and to choose rather to be slaves of matter?

God in His infinite goodness has exalted us to so much   9 honor, and has made us masters over the material world. Shall we then become her slaves? Nay, rather let us claim our birthright, and strive to live the life of the spiritual sons of God. The glorious Sun of Truth has once again risen in the East. From the far horizon of Persia its radiance is spreading far and wide, dispersing the dense clouds of superstition. The light of the unity of mankind is beginning to illumine the world, and soon the banner of Divine harmony and the solidarity of nations will be flying high in the Heavens. Yea, the breezes of the Holy Spirit will inspire the whole world!

Oh, peoples and nations! Arise and work and be happy!   10 Gather together under the tent of the unity of mankind!

35

PAIN AND SORROW

November 22nd

In this world we are influenced by two sentiments, *Joy* and *Pain*. 1

Joy gives us wings! In times of joy our strength is more 2
vital, our intellect keener, and our understanding less clouded.
We seem better able to cope with the world and to find our
sphere of usefulness. But when sadness visits us we become
weak, our strength leaves us, our comprehension is dim and
our intelligence veiled. The actualities of life seem to elude
our grasp, the eyes of our spirits fail to discover the sacred
mysteries, and we become even as dead beings.

There is no human being untouched by these two influences; 3
but all the sorrow and the grief that exist come from the world
of matter—the spiritual world bestows only the joy!

If we suffer it is the outcome of material things, and all the 4
trials and troubles come from this world of illusion.

For instance, a merchant may lose his trade and depression 5
ensues. A workman is dismissed and starvation stares him in
the face. A farmer has a bad harvest, anxiety fills his mind.

A man builds a house which is burnt to the ground and he is straightway homeless, ruined, and in despair.

6   All these examples are to show you that the trials which beset our every step, all our sorrow, pain, shame and grief, are born in the world of matter; whereas the spiritual Kingdom never causes sadness. A man living with his thoughts in this Kingdom knows perpetual joy. The ills all flesh is heir to do not pass him by, but they only touch the surface of his life, the depths are calm and serene.

7   Today, humanity is bowed down with trouble, sorrow and grief, no one escapes; the world is wet with tears; but, thank God, the remedy is at our doors. Let us turn our hearts away from the world of matter and live in the spiritual world! It alone can give us freedom! If we are hemmed in by difficulties we have only to call upon God, and by His great Mercy we shall be helped.

8   If sorrow and adversity visit us, let us turn our faces to the Kingdom and heavenly consolation will be outpoured.

9   If we are sick and in distress let us implore God's healing, and He will answer our prayer.

10   When our thoughts are filled with the bitterness of this world, let us turn our eyes to the sweetness of God's compassion and He will send us heavenly calm! If we are imprisoned in the material world, our spirit can soar into the Heavens and we shall be free indeed!

11   When our days are drawing to a close let us think of the eternal worlds, and we shall be full of joy!

12   You see all round you proofs of the inadequacy of material things—how joy, comfort, peace and consolation are not to be found in the transitory things of the world. Is it not then foolishness to refuse to seek these treasures where they may

be found? The doors of the spiritual Kingdom are open to all, and without is absolute darkness.

Thank God that you in this assembly have this knowledge,   13
for in all the sorrows of life you can obtain supreme consolation. If your days on earth are numbered, you know that everlasting life awaits you. If material anxiety envelops you in a dark cloud, spiritual radiance lightens your path. Verily, those whose minds are illumined by the Spirit of the Most High have supreme consolation.

I myself was in prison forty years—one year alone would   14
have been impossible to bear—nobody survived that imprisonment more than a year! But, thank God, during all those forty years I was supremely happy! Every day, on waking, it was like hearing good tidings, and every night infinite joy was mine. Spirituality was my comfort, and turning to God was my greatest joy. If this had not been so, do you think it possible that I could have lived through those forty years in prison?

Thus, spirituality is the greatest of God's gifts, and "Life   15
Everlasting" means "Turning to God." May you, one and all, increase daily in spirituality, may you be strengthened in all goodness, may you be helped more and more by the Divine consolation, be made free by the Holy Spirit of God, and may the power of the Heavenly Kingdom live and work among you.

This is my earnest desire, and I pray to God to grant you   16
this favor.

36

THE PERFECT HUMAN SENTIMENTS AND VIRTUES

November 23rd

'Abdu'l-Bahá said:

You should all be very happy and thankful to God for the great privilege that is yours. 1

This is purely a spiritual meeting! Praise be to God, your hearts are turned to Him, your souls are attracted to the Kingdom, you have spiritual aspirations, and your thoughts soar above the world of dust. 2

You belong to the world of purity, and are not content to live the life of the animal, spending your days in eating, drinking, and sleeping. You are indeed men! Your thoughts and ambitions are set to acquire human perfection. You live to do good and to bring happiness to others. Your greatest longing is to comfort those who mourn, to strengthen the weak, and to be the cause of hope to the despairing soul. Day and night your thoughts are turned to the Kingdom, and your hearts are full of the Love of God. 3

Thus you know neither opposition, dislike, nor hatred, for every living creature is dear to you and the good of each is sought. 4

5   These are perfect human sentiments and virtues. If a man has none of these, he had better cease to exist. If a lamp has ceased to give light, it had better be destroyed. If a tree bear no fruit, it had better be cut down, for it only cumbereth the ground.

6   Verily, it is better a thousand times for a man to die than to continue living without virtue.

7   We have eyes wherewith to see, but if we do not use them how do they profit us? We have ears wherewith to hear, but if we are deaf of what use are they?

8   We have a tongue wherewith to praise God and proclaim the good tidings, but if we are dumb how useless it is!

9   The All-Loving God created man to radiate the Divine light and to illumine the world by his words, action and life. If he is without virtue he becomes no better than a mere animal, and an animal devoid of intelligence is a vile thing.

10   The Heavenly Father gave the priceless gift of intelligence to man so that he might become a spiritual light, piercing the darkness of materiality, and bringing goodness and truth into the world. If ye will follow earnestly the teachings of Bahá'u'lláh, ye shall indeed become the light of the world, the soul for the body of the world, the comfort and help for humanity, and the source of salvation for the whole universe. Strive therefore, with heart and soul, to follow the precepts of the Blessed Perfection, and rest assured that if ye succeed in living the life he marks out for you, Eternal Life and everlasting joy in the Heavenly Kingdom will be yours, and celestial sustenance will be sent to strengthen you all your days.

11   It is my heartfelt prayer that each one of you may attain to this perfect joy!

37

THE CRUEL INDIFFERENCE OF PEOPLE TOWARDS THE SUFFERING OF FOREIGN RACES

November 24th

'Abdu'l-Bahá said:

I have just been told that there has been a terrible accident 1
in this country. A train has fallen into the river and at least
twenty people have been killed. This is going to be a matter for
discussion in the French Parliament today, and the Director
of the State Railway will be called upon to speak. He will be
cross-examined as to the condition of the railroad and as to
what caused the accident, and there will be a heated argument.
I am filled with wonder and surprise to notice what interest and excitement has been aroused throughout the whole
country on account of the death of twenty people, while
they remain cold and indifferent to the fact that thousands
of Italians, Turks, and Arabs are killed in Tripoli! The horror
of this wholesale slaughter has not disturbed the Government
at all! Yet these unfortunate people are human beings too.

2   Why is there so much interest and eager sympathy shown towards these twenty individuals, while for five thousand persons there is none? They are all men, they all belong to the family of mankind, but they are of other lands and races. It is no concern of the disinterested countries if these men are cut to pieces, this wholesale slaughter does not affect them! How unjust, how cruel is this, how utterly devoid of any good and true feeling! The people of these other lands have children and wives, mothers, daughters, and little sons! In these countries today there is hardly a house free from the sound of bitter weeping, scarcely can one find a home untouched by the cruel hand of war.

3   Alas! we see on all sides how cruel, prejudiced and unjust is man, and how slow he is to believe in God and follow His commandments.

4   If these people would love and help one another instead of being so eager to destroy with sword and cannon, how much nobler would it be! How much better if they would live like a flock of doves in peace and harmony, instead of being like wolves and tearing each other to pieces.

5   Why is man so hard of heart? It is because he does not yet know God. If he had knowledge of God he could not act in direct opposition to His laws; if he were spiritually minded such a line of conduct would be impossible to him. If only the laws and precepts of the prophets of God had been believed, understood and followed, wars would no longer darken the face of the earth.

6   If man had even the rudiments of justice, such a state of things would be impossible.

7   Therefore, I say unto you pray—pray and turn your faces to God, that He, in His infinite compassion and mercy, may

help and succor these misguided ones. Pray that He will grant them spiritual understanding and teach them tolerance and mercy, that the eyes of their minds may be opened and that they may be endued with the gift of the spirit. Then would peace and love walk hand in hand through the lands, and these poor unhappy people might have rest.

Let us all strive night and day to help in the bringing about   8
of better conditions. My heart is broken by these terrible things and cries aloud—may this cry reach other hearts!

Then will the blind see, the dead will be raised, and Justice   9
will come and reign upon the earth.

I beseech you all to pray with heart and soul that this may   10
be accomplished.

38

WE MUST NOT BE DISCOURAGED BY THE SMALLNESS OF OUR NUMBERS

November 25th

When Christ appeared He manifested Himself at Jerusalem. 1
He called men to the Kingdom of God, He invited them to
Eternal Life and He told them to acquire human perfections.
The Light of Guidance was shed forth by that radiant Star,
and He at length gave His life in sacrifice for humanity.

All through His blessed life He suffered oppression and 2
hardship, and in spite of all this humanity was His enemy!

They denied Him, scorned Him, ill-treated Him and 3
cursed Him. He was not treated like a man—and yet in spite
of all this He was the embodiment of pity and of supreme
goodness and love.

He loved all humanity, but they treated Him as an enemy 4
and were incapable of appreciating Him. They set no value on
His words and were not illumined by the flame of His love.

Later they realized who He was; that He was the Sacred 5
and Divine Light, and that His words held Eternal Life.

6   His heart was full of love for all the world, His goodness was destined to reach each one—and as they began to realize these things, they repented—but He had been crucified!

7   It was not until many years after His ascension that they knew who He was, and at the time of His ascension He had only a very few disciples; only a comparatively small following believed His precepts and followed His laws. The ignorant said, "Who is this individual; He has only a few disciples!" But those who knew said: "He is the Sun who will shine in the East and in the West, He is the Manifestation who shall give life to the world."

8   What the first disciples had seen the world realized later.

9   Therefore, you who are in Europe, do not be discouraged because you are few or because people think that your Cause is of no importance. If few people come to your gatherings do not lose heart, and if you are ridiculed and contradicted be not distressed, for the apostles of Christ had the same to bear. They were reviled and persecuted, cursed and ill-treated, but in the end they were victorious and their enemies were found to be wrong.

10   If history should repeat itself and all these same things should happen to you, do not be saddened but be full of joy, and thank God that you are called upon to suffer as holy men of old suffered. If they oppose you be gentle with them, if they contradict be firm in your faith, if they desert you and flee from before you, seek them out and treat them kindly. Do harm to nobody; pray for all; try to make your light shine in the world and let your banner fly high in the Heavens. The beautiful perfume of your noble lives will permeate everywhere. The light of truth kindled in your hearts will shine out to the distant horizon!

The indifference and scorn of the world matters not at all, 11
whereas your lives will be of the greatest importance.

All those who seek truth in the Heavenly Kingdom shine 12
like the stars; they are like fruit trees laden with choice fruit,
like seas full of precious pearls.

Only have faith in the Mercy of God, and spread the 13
Divine Truth.

39

WORDS SPOKEN BY 'ABDU'L-BAHÁ IN PASTOR WAGNER'S CHURCH (FOYER DE L'AME) IN PARIS

November 26th

I am deeply touched by the sympathetic words which have been addressed to me, and I hope that day by day true love and affection may grow among us. God has willed that love should be a vital force in the world, and you all know how I rejoice to speak of love. 1

All down the ages the prophets of God have been sent into the world to serve the cause of truth—Moses brought the law of truth, and all the prophets of Israel after him sought to spread it. 2

When Jesus came He lighted the flaming torch of truth, and carried it aloft so that the whole world might be illumined thereby. After Him came His chosen apostles, and they went far and wide, carrying the light of their Master's teaching into a dark world—and, in their turn, passed on. 3

Then came Muḥammad, who in His time and way spread the knowledge of truth among a savage people; for this has always been the mission of God's elect. 4

149

5   So, at last, when Bahá'u'lláh arose in Persia, this was His most ardent desire, to rekindle the waning light of truth in all lands. All the holy ones of God have tried with heart and soul to spread the light of love and unity throughout the world, so that the darkness of materiality might disappear and the light of spirituality might shine forth among the children of men. Then would hate, slander and murder disappear, and in their stead love, unity and peace would reign.

6   All the Manifestations of God came with the same purpose, and they have all sought to lead men into the paths of virtue. Yet we, their servants, still dispute among ourselves! Why is it thus? Why do we not love one another and live in unity?

7   It is because we have shut our eyes to the underlying principle of all religions, that God is one, that He is the Father of us all, that we are all immersed in the ocean of His mercy and sheltered and protected by His loving care.

8   The glorious Sun of Truth shines for all alike, the waters of Divine Mercy immerse each one, and His Divine favor is bestowed on all His children.

9   This loving God desires peace for all His creatures—why, then, do they spend their time in war?

10   He loves and protects all His children—why do they forget Him?

11   He bestows His Fatherly care on us all—why do we neglect our brothers?

12   Surely, when we realize how God loves and cares for us, we should so order our lives that we may become more like Him.

13   God has created us, one and all—why do we act in opposition to His wishes, when we are all His children, and love the same Father? All these divisions we see on all sides, all these disputes and opposition, are caused because men

cling to *ritual* and outward observances, and forget the simple, underlying truth. It is the *outward practices* of religion that are so different, and it is they that cause disputes and enmity—while the *reality* is always the same, and one. The Reality is the Truth, and truth has no division. Truth is God's guidance, it is the light of the world, it is love, it is mercy. These attributes of truth are also human virtues inspired by the Holy Spirit.

So let us one and all hold fast to truth, and we shall be free indeed! 14

The day is coming when all the religions of the world will unite, for in principle they are one already. There is no need for division, seeing that it is only the outward forms that separate them. Among the sons of men some souls are suffering through ignorance, let us hasten to teach them; others are like children needing care and education until they are grown, and some are sick—to these we must carry Divine healing. 15

Whether ignorant, childish or sick, they must be loved and helped, and not disliked because of their imperfection. 16

Doctors of religion were instituted to bring spiritual healing to the peoples and to be the cause of unity among the nations. If they become the cause of division they had better not exist! A remedy is given to cure a disease, but if it only succeeds in aggravating the complaint, it is better to leave it alone. If religion is only to be a cause of disunion it had better not exist. 17

All the Divine Manifestations sent by God into the world would have gone through their terrible hardships and sufferings for the single hope of spreading Truth, unity and concord among men. Christ endured a life of sorrow, pain and grief, to bring a perfect example of love into the world—and in 18 spite of this we continue to act in a contrary spirit one towards the other!

19   Love is the fundamental principle of God's purpose for man, and He has commanded us to love each other even as He loves us. All these discords and disputes which we hear on all sides only tend to increase materiality.

20   The world for the most part is sunk in materialism, and the blessings of the Holy Spirit are ignored. There is so little real spiritual feeling, and the progress of the world is for the most part merely material. Men are becoming like unto beasts that perish, for we know that they have no spiritual feeling—they do not turn to God, they have no religion! These things belong to man alone, and if he is without them he is a prisoner of nature, and no whit better than an animal.

21   How can man be content to lead only an animal existence when God has made him so high a creature? All creation is made subject to the laws of nature, but man has been able to conquer these laws. The sun, in spite of its power and glory, is bound by the laws of nature, and cannot change its course by so much as a hair's breadth. The great and mighty ocean is powerless to change the ebb and flow of its tides—nothing can stand against nature's laws but man!

22   But to man God has given such wonderful power that he can guide, control and overcome nature.

23   The natural law for man is to walk on the earth, but he makes ships and flies in the air! He is created to live on dry land, but he rides on the sea and even travels under it!

24   He has learnt to control the power of electricity, and he takes it at his will and imprisons it in a lamp! The human voice is made to speak across short distances, but man's power is such that he has made instruments and can speak from

East to West! All these examples show you how man can govern nature, and how, as it were, he wrests a sword from the hand of nature and uses it against herself. Seeing that man has been created master of nature, how foolish it is of him to become her slave! What ignorance and stupidity it is to worship and adore nature, when God in His goodness has made us masters thereof. God's power is visible to all, yet men shut their eyes and see it not. The Sun of Truth is shining in all His splendor, but man with fast shut eyes cannot behold His glory! It is my earnest prayer to God that by His Mercy and Loving Kindness you may all be united, and filled with the utmost joy.

I beseech you, one and all, to add your prayers to mine 25 to the end that war and bloodshed may cease, and that love, friendship, peace and unity may reign in the world.

All down the ages we see how blood has stained the surface 26 of the earth; but now a ray of greater light has come, man's intelligence is greater, spirituality is beginning to grow, and a time is surely coming when the religions of the world will be at peace. Let us leave the discordant arguments concerning outward forms, and let us join together to hasten forward the Divine Cause of unity, until all humanity knows itself to be one family, joined together in love.

PART II

The Eleven Principles out of the Teaching of Bahá'u'lláh,
Explained by 'Abdu'l-Bahá in Paris.

The Search after Truth.
The Unity of Mankind.
Religion ought to be the Cause of Love and Affection
(Not given separately).
The Unity of Religion and Science.
Abolition of Prejudices.
Equalization of Means of Existence.
Equality of Men before the Law.
Universal Peace.
Noninterference of Religion and Politics.
Equality of Sex—Education of Women.
The Power of the Holy Spirit.

40

THEOSOPHICAL SOCIETY, PARIS

Since my arrival in Paris, I have been told of the Theosophi-   1
cal Society, and I know that it is composed of honored and
respected men. You are men of intellect and thought, men
with spiritual ideals, and it is a great pleasure for me to be
among you.

Let us thank God who has drawn us together this evening.   2
It gives me great joy, for I see that you are seekers after truth.
You are not held in bondage by the chains of prejudice, and
your greatest longing is to know the truth. Truth may be likened to the sun! The sun is the luminous body that disperses
all shadows; in the same way does truth scatter the shadows of
our imagination. As the sun gives life to the body of humanity
so does truth give life to their souls. Truth is a sun that rises
from different points on the horizon.

Sometimes the sun rises from the center of the horizon,   3
then in summer it rises farther north, in winter farther
south—but it is always the self-same sun, however different
are the points of its rising.

In like manner truth is one, although its manifestations   4
may be very different. Some men have eyes and see. These

worship the sun, no matter from which point on the horizon it may dawn; and when the sun has left the winter sky to appear in the summer one, they know how to find it again. Others there are who worship only the spot from which the sun arose, and when it arises in its glory from another place they remain in contemplation before the spot of its former rising. Alas! these men are deprived of the blessings of the sun. Those who in truth adore the sun itself will recognize it from whatsoever dawning-place it may appear, and will straightway turn their faces towards its radiance.

5   We must adore the sun itself and not merely the place of its appearance. In the same way men of enlightened heart worship truth on whatever horizon it appears. They are not bound by personality, but they follow the truth, and are able to recognize it no matter from whence it may come. It is this same truth which helps humanity to progress, which gives life to all created beings, for it

6   is the Tree of Life!

In His teaching Bahá'u'lláh gives us the explanation of truth, and I wish to speak to you briefly about this, for I see that you are capable of understanding.

7

The first principle of Bahá'u'lláh is:
The Search for Truth

8

Man must cut himself free from all prejudice and from the result of his own imagination, so that he may be able to search for truth unhindered. Truth is one in all religions, and

9   by means of it the unity of the world can be realized.

All the peoples have a fundamental belief in common. Being one, truth cannot be divided, and the differences that appear to exist among the nations only result from their attachment to prejudice. If only men would search out truth, they would find themselves united.

The second principle of Bahá'u'lláh is: 10
The Unity of Mankind

The one all-loving God bestows His divine Grace and   11 Favor on all mankind; one and all are servants of the Most High, and His Goodness, Mercy and loving Kindness are showered upon all His creatures. The glory of humanity is the heritage of each one.

All men are the leaves and fruit of one same tree, they are   12 all branches of the tree of Adam, they all have the same origin. The same rain has fallen upon them all, the same warm sun makes them grow, they are all refreshed by the same breeze. The only differences that exist and that keep them apart are these: there are the children who need guidance, the ignorant to be instructed, the sick to be tended and healed; thus, I say that the whole of humanity is enveloped by the Mercy and Grace of God. As the Holy Writings tell us: All men are equal before God. He is no respecter of persons.

The third principle of Bahá'u'lláh is: 13
Religion should be the Cause of Love and Affection

Religion should unite all hearts and cause wars and disputes   14 to vanish from the face of the earth, give birth to spirituality, and bring life and light to each heart. If religion becomes a cause of dislike, hatred and division, it were better to be without it, and to withdraw from such a religion would be a truly religious act. For it is clear that the purpose of a remedy is to cure; but if the remedy should only aggravate the complaint it had better be left alone. Any religion which is not a cause of love and unity is no religion. All the holy prophets were as doctors to the soul; they gave prescriptions for the healing of mankind; thus any remedy that causes disease does not come from the great and supreme Physician.

15   The fourth principle of Bahá'u'lláh is:
       The Unity of Religion and Science

16   We may think of science as one wing and religion as the other; a bird needs two wings for flight, one alone would be useless. Any religion that contradicts science or that is opposed to it, is only ignorance—for ignorance is the opposite of knowledge.

17   Religion which consists only of rites and ceremonies of prejudice is not the truth. Let us earnestly endeavor to be the means of uniting religion and science.

18   'Alí, the son-in-law of Muḥammad, said: "That which is in conformity with science is also in conformity with religion." Whatever the intelligence of man cannot understand, religion ought not to accept. Religion and science walk hand in hand, and any religion contrary to science is not the truth.

19   The fifth principle of Bahá'u'lláh is:
       Prejudices of Religion, Race or Sect destroy
       the foundation of Humanity

20   All the divisions in the world, hatred, war and bloodshed, are caused by one or other of these prejudices.

21   The whole world must be looked upon as one single country, all the nations as one nation, all men as belonging to one race. Religions, races, and nations are all divisions of man's making only, and are necessary only in his thought; before

God there are neither Persians, Arabs, French nor English; God is God for all, and to Him all creation is one. We must obey God, and strive to follow Him by leaving all our prejudices and bringing about peace on earth.

The sixth principle of Bahá'u'lláh is: 22
Equal opportunity of the means of Existence

Every human being has the right to live; they have a right   23 to rest, and to a certain amount of well-being. As a rich man is able to live in his palace surrounded by luxury and the greatest comfort, so should a poor man be able to have the necessaries of life. Nobody should die of hunger; everybody should have sufficient clothing; one man should not live in excess while another has no possible means of existence.

Let us try with all the strength we have to bring about   24 happier conditions, so that no single soul may be destitute.

The seventh principle of Bahá'u'lláh is: 25
The Equality of Men—equality before the Law

The *Law* must reign, and not the individual; thus will the   26 world become a place of beauty and true brotherhood will be realized. Having attained solidarity, men will have found truth.

The eighth principle of Bahá'u'lláh is: 27
Universal Peace

A Supreme Tribunal shall be elected by the peoples and gov-   28 ernments of every nation, where members from each country and government shall assemble in unity. All disputes shall be brought before this Court, its mission being to prevent war.

29   The ninth principle of Bahá'u'lláh is:
      That Religion should not concern itself
      with Political Questions

30   Religion is concerned with things of the spirit, politics
      with things of the world. Religion has to work with the world
      of thought, whilst the field of politics lies with the world of
      external conditions.

31   It is the work of the clergy to educate the people, to in-
      struct them, to give them good advice and teaching so that
      they may progress spiritually. With political questions they
      have nothing to do.

32   The tenth principle of Bahá'u'lláh is:
      Education and Instruction of Women

33   Women have equal rights with men upon earth; in religion
      and society they are a very important element. As long as
      women are prevented from attaining their highest possibilities,
      so long will men be unable to achieve the greatness which
      might be theirs.

34   The eleventh principle of Bahá'u'lláh is:
      The Power of the Holy Spirit, by which alone
      Spiritual Development is achieved

35   It is only by the breath of the Holy Spirit that spiritual
      development can come about. No matter how the material
      world may progress, no matter how splendidly it may adorn
      itself, it can never be anything but a lifeless body unless the
      soul is within, for it is the soul that animates the body; the
      body alone has no real significance. Deprived of the blessings
      of the Holy Spirit the material body would be inert.

Here are, very briefly explained, some of the principles of   36
Bahá'u'lláh.

In short, it behooves us all to be lovers of truth. Let us   37
seek her in every season and in every country, being careful
never to attach ourselves to personalities. Let us see the light
wherever it shines, and may we be enabled to recognize the
light of truth no matter where it may arise. Let us inhale the
perfume of the rose from the midst of thorns which surround
it; let us drink the running water from every pure spring.

Since I arrived in Paris, it has given me much pleasure to   38
meet such Parisians as you are, for praise be to God, you are
intelligent, unprejudiced, and you long to know the truth.
You have in your hearts the love of humanity, and as far as
you are able, you exert yourselves in the cause of charitable
work and in the bringing about of unity; this is especially
what Bahá'u'lláh desired.

It is for this reason that I am so happy to be among you,   39
and I pray for you, that you may be receptacles for the Blessings of God, and that you may be the means of spreading
spirituality throughout this country.

You already have a wonderful material civilization and in   40
like manner shall spiritual civilization be yours.

Monsieur Bleck thanked 'Abdu'l-Bahá, and He replied:

"I am very grateful to you for the kind sentiments which   41
you have just uttered. I hope that these two movements will
erelong be spread all over the earth. Then will the unity of
humanity have pitched its tent in the center of the world."

41

THE FIRST PRINCIPLE—
SEARCH AFTER TRUTH

4 Avenue de Camoëns, Paris,
November 10th

The first principle of the Teaching of Bahá'u'lláh is: 1
The Search after Truth

If a man would succeed in his search after truth, he must,   2
in the first place, shut his eyes to all the traditional superstitions of the past.

The Jews have traditional superstitions, the Buddhists   3
and the Zoroastrians are not free from them, neither are the
Christians! All religions have gradually become bound by
tradition and dogma.

All consider themselves, respectively, the only guardians   4
of the truth, and that every other religion is composed of
errors. They themselves are right, all others are wrong! The
Jews believe that they are the only possessors of the truth and
condemn all other religions. The Christians affirm that their
religion is the only true one, that all others are false. Likewise
the Buddhists and Muḥammadans; all limit themselves. If all
condemn one another, where shall we search for truth? All

contradicting one another, all cannot be true. If each believe his particular religion to be the only true one, he blinds his eyes to the truth in the others. If, for instance, a Jew is bound by the external practice of the religion of Israel, he does not permit himself to perceive that truth *can* exist in any other religion; it must be *all* contained in his own!

5   We should, therefore, detach ourselves from the external forms and practices of religion. We must realize that these forms and practices, however beautiful, are but garments clothing the warm heart and the living limbs of Divine truth. We must abandon the prejudices of tradition if we would succeed in finding the truth at the core of all religions. If a Zoroastrian believes that the Sun is God, how can he be united to other religions? While idolaters believe in their various idols, how can they understand the oneness of God?

6   It is, therefore, clear that in order to make any progress in the search after truth we must relinquish superstition. If all seekers would follow this principle they would obtain a clear vision of the truth.

7   If five people meet together to seek for truth, they must begin by cutting themselves free from all their own special conditions and renouncing all preconceived ideas. In order to find truth we must give up our prejudices, our own small trivial notions; an open receptive mind is essential. If our chalice is full of self, there is no room in it for the water of life. The fact that we imagine ourselves to be right and everybody else wrong is the greatest of all obstacles in the path towards unity, and unity is necessary if we would reach truth, for truth is *one*.

8   Therefore it is imperative that we should renounce our own particular prejudices and superstitions if we earnestly desire

to seek the truth. Unless we make a distinction in our minds between dogma, superstition and prejudice on the one hand, and truth on the other, we cannot succeed. When we are in earnest in our search for anything we look for it everywhere. This principle we must carry out in our search for truth.

Science must be accepted. No one truth can contradict another truth. Light is good in whatsoever lamp it is burning! A rose is beautiful in whatsoever garden it may bloom! A star has the same radiance if it shines from the East or from the West. Be free from prejudice, so will you love the Sun of Truth from whatsoever point in the horizon it may arise! You will realize that if the Divine light of truth shone in Jesus Christ it also shone in Moses and in Buddha. The earnest seeker will arrive at this truth. This is what is meant by the "Search after Truth." 9

It means, also, that we must be willing to clear away all that we have previously learned, all that would clog our steps on the way to truth; we must not shrink if necessary from beginning our education all over again. We must not allow our love for any one religion or any one personality to so blind our eyes that we become fettered by superstition! When we are freed from all these bonds, seeking with liberated minds, then shall we be able to arrive at our goal. 10

"Seek the truth, the truth shall make you free." So shall we see the truth in all religions, for truth is in all and truth is one! 11

42

THE SECOND PRINCIPLE— THE UNITY OF MANKIND

November 11th

I spoke yesterday of the first principle of the Teaching of   1
Bahá'u'lláh, "The Search for Truth"; how it is necessary for a
man to put aside all in the nature of superstition, and every
tradition which would blind his eyes to the existence of truth
in all religions. He must not, while loving and clinging to
one form of religion, permit himself to detest all others. It is
essential that he search for truth in all religions, and, if his
seeking be in earnest, he will assuredly succeed.

Now the first discovery which we make in our "Search   2
after Truth," will lead us to the second principle, which is the
"Unity of Mankind." All men are servants of the One God.
One God reigns over all the nations of the world and has
pleasure in all His children. All men are of one family; the
crown of humanity rests on the head of every human being.

In the eyes of the Creator all His children are equal; His   3
goodness is poured forth on all. He does not favor this nation
nor that nation, all alike are His creatures. This being so, why
should we make divisions, separating one race from another?

Why should we create barriers of superstition and tradition bringing discord and hatred among the people?

4   The only difference between members of the human family is that of degree. Some are like children who are ignorant, and must be educated until they arrive at maturity. Some are like the sick and must be treated with tenderness and care. None are bad or evil! We must not be repelled by these poor children. We must treat them with great kindness, teaching the ignorant and tenderly nursing the sick.

5   Consider: Unity is necessary to existence. Love is the very cause of life; on the other hand, separation brings death. In the world of material creation, for instance, all things owe their actual life to unity. The elements which compose wood, mineral, or stone, are held together by the law of attraction. If this law should cease for one moment to operate these elements would not hold together, they would fall apart, and the object would in that particular form cease to exist. The law of attraction has brought together certain elements in the form of this beautiful flower, but when that attraction is withdrawn from this center the flower will decompose, and, as a flower, cease to exist.

6   So it is with the great body of humanity. The wonderful Law of Attraction, Harmony and Unity, holds together this marvelous Creation.

7   As with the whole, so with the parts; whether a flower or a human body, when the attracting principle is withdrawn from it, the flower or the man dies. It is therefore clear that attraction, harmony, unity and Love, are the cause of life, whereas repulsion, discord, hatred and separation bring death.

We have seen that whatever brings division into the world 8
of existence causes death. Likewise in the world of the spirit
does the same law operate.

Therefore should every servant of the One God be obedient 9
to the law of love, avoiding all hatred, discord, and strife. We
find when we observe nature, that the gentler animals group
themselves together into flocks and herds, whereas the savage,
ferocious creatures, such as the lion, the tiger, and the wolf,
live in wild forests, apart from civilization. Two wolves, or two
lions, may live amicably together; but a thousand lambs may
share the same fold and a large number of deer can form one
herd. Two eagles can dwell in the same place, but a thousand
doves can gather into one habitation.

Man should, at least, be numbered among the gentler 10
animals; but when he becomes ferocious he is more cruel
and malicious than the most savage of the animal creation!

Now Bahá'u'lláh has proclaimed the "Unity of the World 11
of Mankind." All peoples and nations are of one family,
the children of one Father, and should be to one another as
brothers and sisters! I hope that you will endeavor in your
lives to show forth and spread this teaching.

Bahá'u'lláh said that we should love even our enemies 12
and be to them as friends. If all men were obedient to this
principle, the greatest unity and understanding would be
established in the hearts of mankind.

43

THE THIRD PRINCIPLE— LOVE AND AFFECTION

[*"That religion ought to be a Cause of Love and Affection"* is much emphasized in many of the Discourses of which the Notes are given in this book, as well as in the explanation of several of the other Principles.]

44

THE FOURTH PRINCIPLE— THE ACCEPTANCE OF THE RELATION BETWEEN RELIGION AND SCIENCE

4 Avenue de Camoëns, Paris,
November 12th

'Abdu'l-Bahá said:

I have spoken to you of some of the principles of Bahá'- 1
u'lláh: *The Search after Truth* and *The Unity of Mankind.* I
will now explain the *Fourth Principle,* which is *The Acceptance*
of the Relation between Religion and Science.

There is no contradiction between true religion and sci- 2
ence. When a religion is opposed to science it becomes mere
superstition: that which is contrary to knowledge is ignorance.

How can a man believe to be a fact that which science has 3
proved to be impossible? If he believes in spite of his reason, it
is rather ignorant superstition than faith. The true principles
of all religions are in conformity with the teachings of science.

The Unity of God is logical, and this idea is not antago- 4
nistic to the conclusions arrived at by scientific study.

5   All religions teach that we must do good, that we must be generous, sincere, truthful, law-abiding, and faithful; all this is reasonable, and logically the only way in which humanity can progress.

6   All religious laws conform to reason, and are suited to the people for whom they are framed, and for the age in which they are to be obeyed.

7   Religion has two main parts:

8   (1) The Spiritual.

9   (2) The Practical.

10   The spiritual part never changes. All the Manifestations of God and His Prophets have taught the same truths and given the same spiritual law. They all teach the one code of morality. There is no division in the truth. The Sun has sent forth many rays to illumine human intelligence, the light is always the same.

11   The practical part of religion deals with exterior forms and ceremonies, and with modes of punishment for certain offences. This is the material side of the law, and guides the customs and manners of the people.

12   In the time of Moses, there were ten crimes punishable by death. When Christ came this was changed; the old axiom "an eye for an eye, and a tooth for a tooth" was converted into "Love your enemies, do good to them that hate you," the stern old law being changed into one of love, mercy and forbearance!

13   In the former days the punishment for theft was the cutting off of the right hand; in our time this law could not be so applied. In this age, a man who curses his father is allowed to live, when formerly he would have been put to death. It is therefore evident that whilst the spiritual law never alters, the

practical rules must change their application with the necessities of the time. The spiritual aspect of religion is the greater, the more important of the two, and this is the same for all time. It never changes! It is the same, yesterday, today, and forever! "As it was the beginning, is now, and ever shall be."

Now, all questions of morality contained in the spiritual,   14
immutable law of every religion are logically right. If religion were contrary to logical reason then it would cease to be a religion and be merely a tradition. Religion and science are the two wings upon which man's intelligence can soar into the heights, with which the human soul can progress. It is not possible to fly with one wing alone! Should a man try to fly with the wing of religion alone he would quickly fall into the quagmire of superstition, whilst on the other hand, with the wing of science alone he would also make no progress, but fall into the despairing slough of materialism. All religions of the present day have fallen into superstitious practices, out of harmony alike with the true principles of the teaching they represent and with the scientific discoveries of the time. Many religious leaders have grown to think that the importance of religion lies mainly in the adherence to a collection of certain dogmas and the practice of rites and ceremonies! Those whose souls they profess to cure are taught to believe likewise, and these cling tenaciously to the outward forms, confusing them with the inward truth.

Now, these forms and rituals differ in the various churches   15
and amongst the different sects, and even contradict one another; giving rise to discord, hatred, and disunion. The outcome of all this dissension is the belief of many cultured men that religion and science are contradictory terms, that religion needs no powers of reflection, and should in no wise

be regulated by science, but must of necessity be opposed, the one to the other. The unfortunate effect of this is that science has drifted apart from religion, and religion has become a mere blind and more or less apathetic following of the precepts of certain religious teachers, who insist on their own favorite dogmas being accepted even when they are contrary to science. This is foolishness, for it is quite evident that science is the light, and, being so, religion *truly* so-called does not oppose knowledge.

16   We are familiar with the phrases "Light and Darkness," "Religion and Science." But the religion which does not walk hand in hand with science is itself in the darkness of superstition and ignorance.

17   Much of the discord and disunion of the world is created by these man-made oppositions and contradictions. If religion were in harmony with science and they walked together, much of the hatred and bitterness now bringing misery to the human race would be at an end.

18   Consider what it is that singles man out from among created beings, and makes of him a creature apart. Is it not his reasoning power, his intelligence? Shall he not make use of these in his study of religion? I say unto you: weigh carefully in the balance of reason and science everything that is presented to you as religion. If it passes this test, then accept it, for it is truth! If, however, it does not so conform, then reject it, for it is ignorance!

19   Look around and see how the world of today is drowned in superstition and outward forms!

20   Some worship the product of their own imagination: they make for themselves an imaginary God and adore this, when the creation of their finite minds cannot be the Infinite Mighty

Maker of all things visible and invisible! Others worship the sun or trees, also stones! In past ages there were those who adored the sea, the clouds, and even clay!

Today, men have grown into such adoring attachment to outward forms and ceremonies that they dispute over this point of ritual or that particular practice, until one hears on all sides of wearisome arguments and unrest. There are individuals who have weak intellects and their powers of reasoning have not developed, but the strength and power of religion must not be doubted because of the incapacity of these persons to understand. 21

A small child cannot comprehend the laws that govern nature, but this is on account of the immature intellect of that child; when he is grown older and has been educated he too will understand the everlasting truths. A child does not grasp the fact that the earth revolves round the sun, but, when his intelligence is awakened, the fact is clear and plain to him. 22

It is impossible for religion to be contrary to science, even though some intellects are too weak or too immature to understand truth. 23

God made religion and science to be the measure, as it were, of our understanding. Take heed that you neglect not such a wonderful power. Weigh all things in this balance. 24

To him who has the power of comprehension religion is like an open book, but how can it be possible for a man devoid of reason and intellectuality to understand the Divine Realities of God? 25

Put all your beliefs into harmony with science; there can be no opposition, for truth is one. When religion, shorn of its superstitions, traditions, and unintelligent dogmas, shows its conformity with science, then will there be a great unify- 26 ing, cleansing force in the world which will sweep before it all wars, disagreements, discords and struggles—and then will mankind be united in the power of the Love of God.

45

THE FIFTH PRINCIPLE—
THE ABOLITION
OF PREJUDICES

4 Avenue de Camoëns, Paris, November 13th

All prejudices, whether of religion, race, politics or nation, must be renounced, for these prejudices have caused the world's sickness. It is a grave malady which, unless arrested, is capable of causing the destruction of the whole human race. Every ruinous war, with its terrible bloodshed and misery, has been caused by one or other of these prejudices. 1

The deplorable wars going on in these days are caused by the fanatical religious hatred of one people for another, or the prejudices of race or color. 2

Until all these barriers erected by prejudice are swept away, it is not possible for humanity to be at peace. For this reason Bahá'u'lláh has said, "These Prejudices are destructive to mankind." 3

Contemplate first the prejudice of religion: consider the nations of so-called religious people; if they were truly worshippers of God they would obey His law which forbids them to kill one another. 4

5   If priests of religion really adored the God of love and served the Divine Light, they would teach their people to keep the chief Commandment, "To be in love and charity with all men." But we find the contrary, for it is often the priests who encourage nations to fight. Religious hatred is ever the most cruel!

6   All religions teach that we should love one another; that we should seek out our own shortcomings before we presume to condemn the faults of others, that we must not consider ourselves superior to our neighbors! We must be careful not to exalt ourselves lest we be humiliated.

7   Who are *we* that we should judge? How shall *we* know who, in the sight of God, is the most upright man? God's thoughts are not like our thoughts! How many men who have seemed saint-like to their friends have fallen into the greatest humiliation. Think of Judas Iscariot; he began well, but remember his end! On the other hand, Paul, the Apostle, was in his early life an enemy of Christ, whilst later he became His most faithful servant. How then can we flatter ourselves and despise others?

8   Let us therefore be humble, without prejudices, preferring others' good to our own! Let us never say, "I am a believer but he is an infidel," "I am near to God, whilst he is an outcast." We can never know what will be the final judgment! Therefore let us help all who are in need of any

9   kind of assistance.

Let us teach the ignorant, and take care of the young child until he grows to maturity. When we find a person fallen into the depths of misery or sin we must be kind to him, take him by the hand, help him to regain his footing, his strength;

we must guide him with love and tenderness, treat him as a friend not as an enemy.

We have no right to look upon any of our fellow-mortals as evil.   10

Concerning the prejudice of race: it is an illusion, a super-   11
stition pure and simple! For God created us all of one race.
There were no differences in the beginning, for we are all
descendants of Adam. In the beginning, also, there were no
limits and boundaries between the different lands; no part
of the earth belonged more to one people than to another. In
the sight of God there is no difference between the various
races. Why should man invent such a prejudice? How can
we uphold war caused by an illusion?

God has not created men that they should destroy one   12
another. All races, tribes, sects and classes share equally in
the Bounty of their Heavenly Father.

The only difference lies in the degree of faithfulness, of   13
obedience to the laws of God. There are some who are as
lighted torches, there are others who shine as stars in the sky
of humanity. The lovers of mankind, these are the superior
men, of whatever nation, creed, or color they may be. For it is
they to whom God will say these blessed words, "Well done,
My good and faithful servants." In that day He will not ask,
"Are you English, French, or perhaps Persian? Do you come
from the East, or from the West?"

The only division that is real is this: There are heavenly   14
men and earthly men; self-sacrificing servants of humanity
in the love of the Most High, bringing harmony and unity,
teaching peace and goodwill to men. On the other hand there
are those selfish men, haters of their brethren, in whose hearts

prejudice has replaced loving kindness, and whose influence breeds discord and strife.

15   To which race or to which color belong these two divisions of men, to the White, to the Yellow, to the Black, to the East or to the West, to the North or to the South? If these are God's divisions, why should we invent others? Political prejudice is equally mischievous, it is one of the greatest causes of bitter strife amongst the children of men. There are people who find pleasure in breeding discord, who constantly endeavor to goad their country into making war upon other nations—and why? They think to advantage their own country to the detriment of all others. They send armies to harass and destroy the land, in order to become famous in the world, for the joy of conquest. That it may be said: "Such a country has defeated another, and brought it under the yoke of their stronger, more superior rule." This victory, bought at the price of much bloodshed, is not lasting! The conqueror shall one day be conquered; and the vanquished ones victorious! Remember the history of the past: did not France conquer Germany more than once—then did not the German nation overcome France?

16   We learn also that France conquered England; then was the English nation victorious over France!

17   These glorious conquests are so ephemeral! Why attach so great importance to them and to their fame, as to be willing to shed the blood of the people for their attainment? Is any victory worth the inevitable train of evils consequent upon human slaughter, the grief and sorrow and ruin which must overwhelm so many homes of both nations? For it is not possible that one country alone should suffer.

Oh! why will man, the disobedient child of God, who 18
should be an example of the power of the spiritual law, turn
his face away from the Divine Teaching and put all his effort
into destruction and war?

My hope is that in this enlightened century the Divine 19
Light of love will shed its radiance over the whole world,
seeking out the responsive heart's intelligence of every human
being; that the light of the Sun of Truth will lead politicians to
shake off all the claims of prejudice and superstition, and with
freed minds to follow the Policy of God: for Divine Politics
are mighty, man's politics are feeble! God has created all the
world, and bestows His Divine Bounty upon every creature.

Are we not the servants of God? Shall we neglect to follow 20
our Master's Example, and ignore His Commands?

I pray that the Kingdom shall come on Earth, and that 21
all darkness shall be driven away by the effulgence of the
Heavenly Sun.

46

THE SIXTH PRINCIPLE—
MEANS OF EXISTENCE

4 Avenue de Camoëns, Paris

One of the most important principles of the Teaching of   1
Bahá'u'lláh is:

The right of every human being to the daily bread whereby   2
they exist, or the equalization of the means of livelihood.

The arrangements of the circumstances of the people must   3
be such that poverty shall disappear, that everyone, as far as
possible, according to his rank and position, shall share in
comfort and well-being.

We see amongst us men who are overburdened with riches   4
on the one hand, and on the other those unfortunate ones
who starve with nothing; those who possess several stately
palaces, and those who have not where to lay their head.
Some we find with numerous courses of costly and dainty
food; whilst others can scarce find sufficient crusts to keep
them alive. Whilst some are clothed in velvets, furs and fine
linen, others have insufficient, poor and thin garments with
which to protect them from the cold.

5   This condition of affairs is wrong, and must be remedied. Now the remedy must be carefully undertaken. It cannot be done by bringing to pass absolute equality between men.

6   Equality is a chimera! It is entirely impracticable! Even if equality could be achieved it could not continue—and if its existence were possible, the whole order of the world would be destroyed. The law of order must always obtain in the world of humanity. Heaven has so decreed in the creation of man.

7   Some are full of intelligence, others have an ordinary amount of it, and others again are devoid of intellect. In these three classes of men there is order but not equality. How could it be possible that wisdom and stupidity should be equal? Humanity, like a great army, requires a general, captains, under-officers in their degree, and soldiers, each with their own appointed duties. Degrees are absolutely necessary to ensure an orderly organization. An army could not be composed of generals alone, or of captains only, or of nothing but soldiers without one in authority. The certain result of such a plan would be that disorder and demoralization would overtake the whole army.

8   King Lycurgus, the philosopher, made a great plan to equalize the subjects of Sparta; with self-sacrifice and wisdom was the experiment begun. Then the king called the people of his kingdom, and made them swear a great oath to maintain the same order of government if he should leave the country, also that nothing should make them alter it until his return. Having secured this oath, he left his kingdom of Sparta and never returned. Lycurgus abandoned the situation, renouncing his high position, thinking to achieve the permanent good of his country by the equalization of the property and of the conditions of life in his kingdom. All the self-sacrifice

of the king was in vain. The great experiment failed. After a time all was destroyed; his carefully thought-out constitution came to an end.

The futility of attempting such a scheme was shown and the impossibility of attaining equal conditions of existence was proclaimed in the ancient kingdom of Sparta. In our day any such attempt would be equally doomed to failure. 9

Certainly, some being enormously rich and others lamentably poor, an organization is necessary to control and improve this state of affairs. It is important to limit riches, as it is also of importance to limit poverty. Either extreme is not good. To be seated in the mean* is most desirable. If it be right for a capitalist to possess a large fortune, it is equally just that his workman should have a sufficient means of existence. 10

A financier with colossal wealth should not exist whilst near him is a poor man in dire necessity. When we see poverty allowed to reach a condition of starvation it is a sure sign that somewhere we shall find tyranny. Men must bestir themselves in this matter, and no longer delay in altering conditions which bring the misery of grinding poverty to a very large number of the people. The rich must give of their abundance, they must soften their hearts and cultivate a compassionate intelligence, taking thought for those sad ones who are suffering from lack of the very necessities of life. 11

There must be special laws made, dealing with these extremes of riches and of want. The members of the Government should consider the laws of God when they are framing plans for the ruling of the people. The general rights of mankind must be guarded and preserved. 12

* "Give me neither poverty nor riches."—Proverbs 30:8.

13   The government of the countries should conform to the Divine Law which gives equal justice to all. This is the only way in which the deplorable superfluity of great wealth and miserable, demoralizing, degrading poverty can be abolished. Not until this is done will the Law of God be obeyed.

47

THE SEVENTH PRINCIPLE— EQUALITY OF MEN

"The Laws of God are not imposition of will, or of power, 1
or pleasure, but the resolutions of truth, reason and justice."

All men are equal before the law, which must reign 2
absolutely.

The object of punishment is not vengeance, but the pre- 3
vention of crime.

Kings must rule with wisdom and justice; prince, peer and 4
peasant alike have equal rights to just treatment, there must be
no favor shown to individuals. A judge must be no "respecter
of persons," but administer the law with strict impartiality
in every case brought before him.

If a person commit a crime against you, you have not the 5
right to forgive him; but the law must punish him in order to
prevent a repetition of that same crime by others, as the pain
of the individual is unimportant beside the general welfare
of the people.

When perfect justice reigns in every country of the Eastern 6
and Western World, then will the earth become a place of
beauty. The dignity and equality of every servant of God will
be acknowledged; the ideal of the solidarity of the human

race, the true brotherhood of man, will be realized; and the glorious light of the Sun of Truth will illumine the souls of all men.

48

THE EIGHTH PRINCIPLE— UNIVERSAL PEACE

4 Avenue de Camoëns, Paris

A Supreme Tribunal shall be established by the peoples and Governments of every nation, composed of members elected from each country and Government. The members of this Great Council shall assemble in unity. All disputes of an international character shall be submitted to this Court, its work being to arrange by arbitration everything which otherwise would be a cause of war. The mission of this Tribunal would be to prevent war.

One of the great steps towards universal peace would be the establishment of a universal language. Bahá'u'lláh commands that the servants of humanity should meet together, and either choose a language which now exists, or form a new one. This was revealed in the Kitáb-i-Aqdas forty years ago. It is there pointed out that the question of diversity of tongues is a very difficult one. There are more than eight hundred languages in the world, and no person could acquire them all.

195

3   The races of mankind are not isolated as in former days. Now, in order to be in close relationship with all countries it is necessary to be able to speak their tongues.

4   A universal language would make intercourse possible with every nation. Thus it would be needful to know two languages only, the mother tongue and the universal speech. The latter would enable a man to communicate with any and every man in the world!

5   A third language would not be needed. To be able to talk with a member of any race and country without requiring an interpreter, how helpful and restful to all!

6   Esperanto has been drawn up with this end in view: it is a fine invention and a splendid piece of work, but it needs perfecting. Esperanto as it stands is very difficult for some people.

7   An international Congress should be formed, consisting of delegates from every nation in the world, Eastern as well as Western. This Congress should form a language that could be acquired by all, and every country would thereby reap great benefit.

8   Until such a language is in use, the world will continue to feel the vast need of this means of intercourse. Difference of speech is one of the most fruitful causes of dislike and distrust that exists between nations, which are kept apart by their inability to understand each other's language more than by any other reason.

9   If everybody could speak one language, how much more easy would it be to serve humanity!

10   Therefore appreciate "Esperanto," for it is the beginning of the carrying out of one of the most important of the Laws of Bahá'u'lláh, and it must continue to be improved and perfected.

49

THE NINTH PRINCIPLE—
THE NONINTERFERENCE OF
RELIGION WITH POLITICS

4 Avenue de Camoëns, Paris,
November 17th

In the conduct of life, man is actuated by two main motives: 1
"The Hope for Reward" and "The Fear of Punishment."

This hope and this fear must consequently be greatly taken   2
into account by those in authority who have important posts
under Government. Their business in life is to consult together for the framing of laws, and to provide for their just
administration.

The tent of the order of the world is raised and established   3
on the two pillars of "Reward and Retribution."

In despotic Governments carried on by men without Di-   4
vine faith, where no fear of spiritual retribution exists, the
execution of the laws is tyrannical and unjust.

There is no greater prevention of oppression than these   5
two sentiments, hope and fear. They have both political and
spiritual consequences.

6   If administrators of the law would take into consideration the spiritual consequences of their decisions, and follow the guidance of religion, "They would be Divine agents in the world of action, the representatives of God for those who are on earth, and they would defend, for the love of God, the interests of His servants as they would defend their own." If a governor realizes his responsibility, and fears to defy the Divine Law, his judgments will be just. Above all, if he believes that the consequences of his actions will follow him beyond his earthly life, and that "as he sows so must he reap," such a man will surely avoid injustice and tyranny.

7   Should an official, on the contrary, think that all responsibility for his actions must end with his earthly life, knowing and believing nothing of Divine favors and a spiritual kingdom of joy, he will lack the incentive to just dealing, and the inspiration to destroy oppression and unrighteousness.

8   When a ruler knows that his judgments will be weighed in a balance by the Divine Judge, and that if he be not found wanting he will come into the Celestial Kingdom and that the light of the Heavenly Bounty will shine upon him, then will he surely act with justice and equity. Behold how important it is that Ministers of State should be enlightened by religion!

9   With political questions the clergy, however, have nothing to do! Religious matters should not be confused with politics in the present state of the world (for their interests are not identical).

10   Religion concerns matters of the heart, of the spirit, and of morals.

11   Politics are occupied with the material things of life. Religious teachers should not invade the realm of politics; they should concern themselves with the spiritual education of the

people; they should ever give good counsel to men, trying to serve God and humankind; they should endeavor to awaken spiritual aspiration, and strive to enlarge the understanding and knowledge of humanity, to improve morals, and to increase the love for justice.

This is in accordance with the Teaching of Bahá'u'lláh. In the Gospel also it is written, "Render unto Caesar the things which are Caesar's, and unto God the things which are God's." 12

In Persia there are some amongst the important Ministers of State who are religious, who are exemplary, who worship God, and who fear to disobey His Laws, who judge justly and rule their people with Equity. Other Governors there are in this land who have no fear of God before their eyes, who think not of the consequences of their actions, working for their own desires, and these have brought Persia into great trouble and difficulty. 13

Oh, friends of God, be living examples of justice! So that by the Mercy of God, the world may see in your actions that you manifest the attributes of justice and mercy. 14

Justice is not limited, it is a universal quality. Its operation must be carried out in all classes, from the highest to the lowest. Justice must be sacred, and the rights of all the people must be considered. Desire for others only that which you desire for yourselves. Then shall we rejoice in the Sun of Justice, which shines from the Horizon of God. 15

Each man has been placed in a post of honor, which he must not desert. A humble workman who commits an injustice is as much to blame as a renowned tyrant. Thus we all have our choice between justice and injustice. 16

I hope that each one of you will become just, and direct your thoughts towards the unity of mankind; that you will 17 never harm your neighbors nor speak ill of anyone; that you will respect the rights of all men, and be more concerned for the interests of others than for your own. Thus will you become torches of Divine justice, acting in accordance with the Teaching of Bahá'u'lláh, who, during His life, bore innumerable trials and persecutions in order to show forth to the world of mankind the virtues of the World of Divinity, making it possible for you to realize the supremacy of the spirit, and to rejoice in the Justice of God.

18   By His Mercy, the Divine Bounty will be showered upon you, and for this I pray!

50

THE TENTH PRINCIPLE—
EQUALITY OF SEX

4 Avenue de Camoëns, Paris,
November 14th

The Tenth Principle of the teaching of Bahá'u'lláh is the   1
equality of the sexes.

God has created all creatures in couples. Man, beast, or   2
vegetable, all the things of these three kingdoms are of two
sexes, and there is absolute equality between them.

In the vegetable world there are male plants and female   3
plants; they have equal rights, and possess an equal share of
the beauty of their species; though indeed the tree that bears
fruit might be said to be superior to that which is unfruitful.

In the animal kingdom we see that the male and the female   4
have equal rights; and that they each share the advantages of
their kind.

Now in the two lower kingdoms of nature we have seen   5
that there is no question of the superiority of one sex over the
other. In the world of humanity we find a great difference;
the female sex is treated as though inferior, and is not al-

lowed equal rights and privileges. This condition is due not to nature, but to education. In the Divine Creation there is no such distinction. Neither sex is superior to the other in the sight of God. Why then should one sex assert the inferiority of the other, withholding just rights and privileges as though God had given His authority for such a course of action? If women received the same educational advantages as those of men, the result would demonstrate the equality of capacity of both for scholarship.

6   In some respects woman is superior to man. She is more tenderhearted, more receptive, her intuition is more intense.

7   It is not to be denied that in various directions woman at present is more backward than man, also that this temporary inferiority is due to the lack of educational opportunity. In the necessity of life, woman is more instinct with power than man, for to her he owes his very existence.

8   If the mother is educated then her children will be well taught. When the mother is wise, then will the children be led into the path of wisdom. If the mother be religious she will show her children how they should love God. If the mother is moral she guides her little ones into the ways of uprightness.

9   It is clear therefore that the future generation depends on the mothers of today. Is not this a vital responsibility for the woman? Does she not require every possible advantage to equip her for such a task?

10   Therefore, surely, God is not pleased that so important an instrument as woman should suffer from want of training in order to attain the perfections desirable and necessary for her great life's work! Divine Justice demands that the rights of both sexes should be equally respected since neither is superior to the other in the eyes of Heaven. Dignity before

God depends, not on sex, but on purity and luminosity of heart. Human virtues belong equally to all!

Woman must endeavor then to attain greater perfection, 11 to be man's equal in every respect, to make progress in all in which she has been backward, so that man will be compelled to acknowledge her equality of capacity and attainment.

In Europe women have made greater progress than in the 12 East, but there is still much to be done! When students have arrived at the end of their school term an examination takes place, and the result thereof determines the knowledge and capacity of each student. So will it be with woman; her actions will show her power, there will no longer be any need to proclaim it by words.

It is my hope that women of the East, as well as their 13 Western sisters, will progress rapidly until humanity shall reach perfection.

God's Bounty is for all and gives power for all progress. 14 When men own the equality of women there will be no need for them to struggle for their rights! One of the principles then of Bahá'u'lláh is the equality of sex.

Women must make the greatest effort to acquire spiritual 15 power and to increase in the virtue of wisdom and holiness until their enlightenment and striving succeeds in bringing about the unity of mankind. They must work with a burning enthusiasm to spread the Teaching of Bahá'u'lláh among the peoples, so that the radiant light of the Divine Bounty may envelop the souls of all the nations of the world!

51

THE ELEVENTH PRINCIPLE—
THE POWER OF
THE HOLY SPIRIT

4 Avenue de Camoëns, Paris,
November 18th

In the teaching of Bahá'u'lláh, it is written: "By the Power of the Holy Spirit alone is man able to progress, for the power of man is limited and the Divine Power is boundless." The reading of history brings us to the conclusion that all truly great men, the benefactors of the human race, those who have moved men to love the right and hate the wrong and who have caused real progress, all these have been inspired by the force of the Holy Spirit.

1

The Prophets of God have not all graduated in the schools of learned philosophy; indeed they were often men of humble birth, to all appearance ignorant, unknown men of no importance in the eyes of the world; sometimes even lacking the knowledge of reading and writing.

2

That which raised these great ones above men, and by which they were able to become Teachers of the truth, was

3

the power of the Holy Spirit. Their influence on humanity, by virtue of this mighty inspiration, was great and penetrating.

4   The influence of the wisest philosophers, without this Spirit Divine, has been comparatively unimportant, however extensive their learning and deep their scholarship.

5   The unusual intellects, for instance, of Plato, Aristotle, Pliny and Socrates, have not influenced men so greatly that they have been anxious to sacrifice their lives for their teachings; whilst some of those simple men so moved humanity that thousands of men have become willing martyrs to uphold their words; for these words were inspired by the Divine Spirit of God! The prophets of Judah and Israel, Elijah, Jeremiah, Isaiah and Ezekiel, were humble men, as were also the apostles of Jesus Christ.

6   Peter, the chief of the apostles, used to divide the proceeds of his fishing into seven parts, and when, having taken one part for each day's use, he arrived at the seventh portion, he knew it was the Sabbath day. Consider this! and then think of his future position; to what glory he attained because the Holy Spirit wrought great works through him.

7   We understand that the Holy Spirit is the energizing factor in the life of man. Whosoever receives this power is able to influence all with whom he comes into contact.

8   The greatest philosophers without this Spirit are powerless, their souls lifeless, their hearts dead! Unless the Holy Spirit breathes into their souls, they can do no good work. No system of philosophy has ever been able to change the manners and customs of a people for the better. Learned philosophers, unenlightened by the Divine Spirit, have often been men of inferior morality; they have not proclaimed in their actions the reality of their beautiful phrases.

The difference between spiritual philosophers and others is 9 shown by their lives. The Spiritual Teacher shows His belief in His own teaching, by Himself *being* what He recommends to others.

A humble man without learning, but filled with the Holy 10 Spirit, is more powerful than the most nobly-born profound scholar without that inspiration. He who is educated by the Divine Spirit can, in his time, lead others to receive the same Spirit.

I pray for you that you may be informed by the life of the 11 Divine Spirit, so that you may be the means of educating others. The life and morals of a spiritual man are, in themselves, an education to those who know him.

Think not of your own limitations, dwell only on the 12 welfare of the Kingdom of Glory. Consider the influence of Jesus Christ on His apostles, then think of their effect upon the world. These simple men were enabled by the power of the Holy Spirit to spread the glad tidings!

So may you all receive Divine assistance! No capacity is 13 limited when led by the Spirit of God!

The earth of itself has no properties of life, it is barren 14 and dry, until fertilized by the sun and the rain; still the earth need not bewail its own limitations.

May you be given life! May the rain of the Divine Mercy 15 and the warmth of the Sun of Truth make your gardens fruitful, so that many beautiful flowers of exquisite fragrance and love may blossom in abundance. Turn your faces away from the contemplation of your own finite selves and fix your eyes upon the Everlasting Radiance; then will your souls receive in full measure the Divine Power of the Spirit and the Blessings of the Infinite Bounty.

16   If you thus keep yourselves in readiness, you will become
to the world of humanity a burning flame, a star of guidance,
and a fruitful tree, changing all its darkness and woe into light
and joy by the shining of the Sun of Mercy and the infinite
blessings of the Glad Tidings.

17   This is the meaning of the power of the Holy Spirit, which
I pray may be bountifully showered upon you.

52

THIS GREAT AND GLORIOUS CAUSE

4 Avenue de Camoëns, Paris,
November 28th

In these gatherings where we have met and spoken together   1
you have all become acquainted with the principles of this
dispensation, and with the *reality of facts*. Unto you it has
been given to know these things, but there are many still unenlightened and submerged in superstition. They have heard
but little of this great and glorious Cause, and the knowledge
they have is for the most part based only on hearsay. Alas,
poor souls, the knowledge they have is not based on truth, the
foundation of their belief is not the teaching of Bahá'u'lláh!
There is, assuredly, a certain amount of truth in what they
have been told, but for the most part their information has
been inaccurate.

The true principles of the blessed Cause of God are the   2
eleven rules which I have given you, and I have carefully
explained these, one by one.

You must endeavor always to live and act in direct obedi-   3
ence to the teachings and laws of Bahá'u'lláh, so that every

individual may see in all the acts of your life that in word and in deed you are followers of the Blessed Perfection.

4   Exert yourselves so that this glorious teaching may encircle the globe, and that spirituality may be infused into the hearts of men.

5   The breath of the Holy Spirit shall confirm you, and although many will arise against you, they shall not prevail!

6   When the Lord Christ was crowned with thorns, He knew that all the diadems of the world were at His feet. All earthly crowns, however brilliant, powerful and resplendent, bowed in adoration before the crown of thorns! It was from this sure and certain knowledge He spoke, when He said: "All power is given unto Me, in Heaven and in earth."*

7   Now I say unto you, bear this on your hearts and in your minds. Verily your light shall illumine the whole world, your spirituality shall affect the heart of things. You shall in truth become the lighted torches of the globe. Fear not, neither be dismayed, for your light shall penetrate the densest darkness. This is the Promise of God, which I give unto you. Rise! and serve the Power of God!

---

* Matthew 18:18.

53

THE LAST MEETING

15 Rue Greuze, Paris,
December 1st

When I arrived in Paris some time ago for the first time, I looked around me with much interest, and in my mind I likened this beautiful city to a large garden. 1

With loving care and much thought I examined the soil, and found it to be very good and full of possibility for steadfast faith and firm belief, for a seed of God's love has been cast into the ground. 2

Clouds of Heavenly Mercy showered their rain upon it, and the Sun of Truth fell warmly upon the young seeds, and today one can see in your midst the birth of belief. The seed cast into the ground has begun to spring up, and day by day you will see it grow. The bounties of the Kingdom of Bahá'u'lláh shall indeed bring forth a wondrous harvest! 3

Behold! I bring you glad and joyful tidings! Paris will become a garden of roses! All kinds of beautiful flowers will spring up and flourish in this garden, and the fame of their fragrance and beauty will be spread in all lands. When I think of Paris in the future, I seem to see her bathed in the light 4 of the Holy Spirit! Verily, the day is dawning when Paris will receive her illumination, and the Goodness and Mercy of God will be visible to every living creature.

5   Do not allow your minds to dwell on the present, but with eyes of faith look into the future, for in truth the Spirit of God is working in your midst.

6   Since my arrival a few weeks ago, I can see the growth of spirituality. At the beginning only a few souls came to me for Light, but during my short sojourn among you the numbers have increased and doubled. This is a promise for the future!

7   When Christ was crucified and left this world, He had only eleven disciples and a very few followers; but as He served the Cause of truth, look today at the result of His life's work! He has illumined the world, and given life to dead humanity. After His ascension little by little His Cause grew, the souls of His followers became more and more luminous, and the exquisite perfume of their saintly lives spread on all sides.

8   Now today, thank God, a similar condition has begun in Paris. There are many souls who have turned to the Kingdom of God, and who are attracted to unity, love and truth.

9   Try so to work that the goodness and mercy of the Most Glorious may enfold the whole of Paris. The Breath of the Holy Spirit will help you, the Celestial Light of the Kingdom will shine in your hearts, and the blessed angels of God from Heaven will bring you strength and will succor you. Then thank God with all your hearts that you have attained to this supreme benefit. A great part of the world is plunged in sleep, but you have been awakened. Many are blind, but you see!

10 The call of the Kingdom is heard in your midst. Glory be to God, you have been born again, you have been baptized

by the fire of the Love of God; you have been plunged in the Sea of Life and regenerated by the Spirit of Love!

Having received such favor be thankful unto God, and never doubt His Goodness and Loving Kindness but have undying faith in the Bounties of the Kingdom. Consort together in brotherly love, be ready to lay down your lives one for the other, and not only for those who are dear to you, but for all humanity. Look upon the whole human race as members of one family, all children of God; and, in so doing, you will see no difference between them. 11

Humanity may be likened to a tree. This tree has branches, leaves, buds and fruit. Think of all men as being flowers, leaves or buds of this tree, and try to help each and all to realize and enjoy God's blessings. God neglects none: He loves all. 12

The only real difference that exists between people is that they are at various stages of development. Some are imperfect—these must be brought to perfection. Some are asleep—they must be awakened; some are negligent—they must be roused; but one and all are the children of God. Love them all with your whole heart; no one is a stranger to the other, all are friends. Tonight I come to say farewell to you—but bear this in your minds, that although our bodies may be far apart, in spirit we shall always be together. 13

I bear you one and all in my heart, and will forget none of you—and I hope that none of you will forget me. 14

I in the East, and you in the West, let us try with heart and soul that unity may dwell in the world, that all the peoples may become one people, and that the whole surface of the earth may be like one country—for the Sun of Truth shines on all alike. 15

16   All the Prophets of God came for love of this one great aim.

17   Look how Abraham strove to bring faith and love among the people; how Moses tried to unite the people by sound laws; how the Lord Christ suffered unto death to bring the light of love and truth into a darkened world; how Muḥammad sought to bring unity and peace between the various uncivilized tribes among whom He dwelt. And last of all, Bahá'u'lláh has suffered forty years for the same cause—the single noble purpose of spreading love among the children of men—and for the peace and unity of the world the Báb

18   gave up His life.

Thus, strive to follow the example of these Divine Beings, drink from Their fountain, be illumined by Their Light, and to the world be as symbols of the Mercy and Love of God. Be unto the world as rain and clouds of mercy, as suns of truth; be a celestial army, and you shall indeed conquer the

19   city of hearts.

Be thankful unto God that Bahá'u'lláh has given us a firm and solid foundation. He left no place for sadness in hearts, and the writings of His sacred pen contain consolation for the whole world. He had the words of truth, and anything that is contrary to His teaching is false. The chief aim of all

20   His work was to do away with division.

The testament of Bahá'u'lláh is a Rain of Goodness, a Sun of Truth, Water of Life, the Holy Spirit. Thus open your hearts to receive the full power of His Beauty, and I will pray for you all that this joy may be yours.

21   Now I say "Good-bye."

22   This I say only to your outer selves; I do not say it to your souls, for our souls are always together.

Be comforted, and rest assured that day and night I shall 23
turn to the Kingdom of the Most Glorious in supplication
for you, that day by day you may grow better and holier,
nearer to God, and more and more illumined by the radiance
of His Love.

PART III

54

ADDRESS BY 'ABDU'L-BAHÁ AT THE FRIENDS' MEETING HOUSE, ST. MARTIN'S LANE, LONDON, W.C.

Sunday, January 12th, 1913

About one thousand years ago a society was formed in Persia called the Society of the Friends, who gathered together for silent communion with the Almighty. 1

They divided Divine philosophy into two parts: one kind is that of which the knowledge can be acquired through lectures and study in schools and colleges. The second kind of philosophy was that of the Illuminati, or followers of the inner light. The schools of this philosophy were held in silence. Meditating, and turning their faces to the Source of Light, from that central Light the mysteries of the Kingdom were reflected in the hearts of these people. All the Divine problems were solved by this power of illumination. 2

This Society of Friends increased greatly in Persia, and up to the present time their societies exist. Many books and epistles were written by their leaders. When they assemble in their meeting-house they sit silently and contemplate; their 3 leader opens with a certain proposition, and says to the assembly "You must meditate on this problem." Then, freeing their minds from everything else, they sit and reflect, and before long the answer is revealed to them. Many abstruse divine questions are solved by this illumination.

4 Some of the great questions unfolding from the rays of the Sun of Reality upon the mind of man are: the problem of the reality of the spirit of man; of the birth of the spirit; of its birth from this world into the world of God; the question of the inner life of the spirit and of its fate after its ascension from the body.

5 They also meditate upon the scientific questions of the day, and these are likewise solved.

6 These people, who are called "Followers of the inner light," attain to a superlative degree of power, and are entirely freed from blind dogmas and imitations. Men rely on the statements of these people: by themselves—within themselves—they solve all mysteries.

7 If they find a solution with the assistance of the inner light, they accept it, and afterwards they declare it: otherwise they would consider it a matter of blind imitation. They go so far as to reflect upon the essential nature of the Divinity, of the Divine revelation, of the manifestation of the Deity in this world. All the divine and scientific questions are solved by them through the power of the spirit.

8 Bahá'u'lláh says there is a sign (from God) in every phenomenon: the sign of the intellect is contemplation and the sign of contemplation is silence, because it is impossible for a man to do two things at one time—he cannot both speak and meditate.

It is an axiomatic fact that while you meditate you are 9
speaking with your own spirit. In that state of mind you put
certain questions to your spirit and the spirit answers: the
light breaks forth and the reality is revealed.

You cannot apply the name "man" to any being void of 10
this faculty of meditation; without it he would be a mere
animal, lower than the beasts.

Through the faculty of meditation man attains to eternal 11
life; through it he receives the breath of the Holy Spirit—the
bestowal of the Spirit is given in reflection and meditation.

The spirit of man is itself informed and strengthened dur- 12
ing meditation; through it affairs of which man knew nothing
are unfolded before his view. Through it he receives Divine
inspiration, through it he receives heavenly food.

Meditation is the key for opening the doors of mysteries. 13
In that state man abstracts himself: in that state man with-
draws himself from all outside objects; in that subjective
mood he is immersed in the ocean of spiritual life and can
unfold the secrets of things-in-themselves. To illustrate this,
think of man as endowed with two kinds of sight; when
the power of insight is being used the outward power of
vision does not see.

This faculty of meditation frees man from the animal 14
nature, discerns the reality of things, puts man in touch
with God.

This faculty brings forth from the invisible plane the sci- 15
ences and arts. Through the meditative faculty inventions are
made possible, colossal undertakings are carried out; through
it governments can run smoothly. Through this faculty man
enters into the very Kingdom of God.

16 Nevertheless some thoughts are useless to man; they are like waves moving in the sea without result. But if the faculty of meditation is bathed in the inner light and characterized with divine attributes, the results will be confirmed.

17 The meditative faculty is akin to the mirror; if you put it before earthly objects it will reflect them. Therefore if the spirit of man is contemplating earthly subjects he will be informed of these.

18 But if you turn the mirror of your spirits heavenwards, the heavenly constellations and the rays of the Sun of Reality will be reflected in your hearts, and the virtues of the Kingdom will be obtained.

19 Therefore let us keep this faculty rightly directed—turning it to the heavenly Sun and not to earthly objects—so that we may discover the secrets of the Kingdom, and comprehend the allegories of the Bible and the mysteries of the spirit.

20 May we indeed become mirrors reflecting the heavenly realities, and may we become so pure as to reflect the stars of heaven.

55

PRAYER

97 Cadogan Gardens, London,
December 26th, 1912

"Should Prayer take the form of action?"

'Abdu'l-Bahá: "Yes: In the Bahá'í Cause arts, sciences and   1
all crafts are (counted as) worship. The man who makes a
piece of notepaper to the best of his ability, conscientiously,
concentrating all his forces on perfecting it, is giving praise
to God. Briefly, all effort and exertion put forth by man from
the fullness of his heart is worship, if it is prompted by the
highest motives and the will to do service to humanity. This
is worship: to serve mankind and to minister to the needs of
the people. Service is prayer. A physician ministering to the
sick, gently, tenderly, free from prejudice and believing in the
solidarity of the human race, he is giving praise."

"What is the purpose of our lives?"

'Abdu'l-Bahá: "To acquire virtues. We come from the earth;   2
why were we transferred from the mineral to the vegetable
kingdom—from the plant to the animal kingdom? So that

we may attain perfection in each of these kingdoms, that we may possess the best qualities of the mineral, that we may acquire the power of growing as in the plant, that we may be adorned with the instincts of the animal and possess the faculties of sight, hearing, smell, touch and taste, until from the animal kingdom we step into the world of humanity and are gifted with reason, the power of invention, and the forces of the spirit."

56

EVIL

"What is evil?"

'Abdu'l-Bahá: "Evil is imperfection. Sin is the state of man   1
in the world of the baser nature, for in nature exist defects
such as injustice, tyranny, hatred, hostility, strife: these are
characteristics of the lower plane of nature. These are the
sins of the world, the fruits of the tree from which Adam did
eat. Through education we must free ourselves from these
imperfections. The Prophets of God have been sent, the Holy
Books have been written, so that man may be made free. Just
as he is born into this world of imperfection from the womb
of his earthly mother, so is he born into the world of spirit
through divine education. When a man is born into the world
of phenomena he finds the universe; when he is born from
this world to the world of the spirit, he finds the Kingdom."

57

THE PROGRESS OF THE SOUL

"Does the soul progress more through sorrow or through the joy in this world?"

'Abdu'l-Bahá: "The mind and spirit of man advance when   1
he is tried by suffering. The more the ground is ploughed
the better the seed will grow, the better the harvest will be.
Just as the plough furrows the earth deeply, purifying it of
weeds and thistles, so suffering and tribulation free man
from the petty affairs of this worldly life until he arrives at
a state of complete detachment. His attitude in this world
will be that of divine happiness. Man is, so to speak, unripe:
the heat of the fire of suffering will mature him. Look back
to the times past and you will find that the greatest men
have suffered most."

*"He who through suffering has attained development, should
he fear happiness?"*

'Abdu'l-Bahá: "Through suffering he will attain to an eternal   2
happiness which nothing can take from him. The apostles of
Christ suffered: they attained eternal happiness."

"Then it is impossible to attain happiness without suffering?"

3 *Abdu'l-Bahá:* "To attain eternal happiness one must suffer. He who has reached the state of self-sacrifice has true joy. Temporal joy will vanish."

"Can a departed soul converse with someone still on earth?"

4 *Abdu'l-Bahá:* "A conversation can be held, but not as our conversation. There is no doubt that the forces of the higher worlds interplay with the forces of this plane. The heart of man is open to inspiration; this is spiritual communication. As in a dream one talks with a friend while the mouth is silent, so is it in the conversation of the spirit. A man may converse with the ego within him saying: 'May I do this? Would it be advisable for me to do this work?' Such as this is conversation with the higher self."

58

THE FOUR KINDS OF LOVE

97 Cadogan Gardens, London,
Saturday, January 4th, 1913

What a power is love! It is the most wonderful, the greatest   1
of all living powers.

Love gives life to the lifeless. Love lights a flame in the heart   2
that is cold. Love brings hope to the hopeless and gladdens
the hearts of the sorrowful.

In the world of existence there is indeed no greater power   3
than the power of love. When the heart of man is aglow with
the flame of love, he is ready to sacrifice all—even his life. In
the Gospel it is said God is love.

There are four kinds of love. The first is the love that flows   4
from God to man; it consists of the inexhaustible graces, the
Divine effulgence and heavenly illumination. Through this
love the world of being receives life. Through this love man
is endowed with physical existence, until, through the breath
of the Holy Spirit—this same love—he receives eternal life
and becomes the image of the Living God. This love is the
origin of all the love in the world of creation.

5   The second is the love that flows from man to God. This is faith, attraction to the Divine, enkindlement, progress, entrance into the Kingdom of God, receiving the Bounties of God, illumination with the lights of the Kingdom. This love is the origin of all philanthropy; this love causes the hearts of men to reflect the rays of the Sun of Reality.

6   The third is the love of God towards the Self or Identity of God. This is the transfiguration of His Beauty, the reflection of Himself in the mirror of His Creation. This is the reality of love, the Ancient Love, the Eternal Love. Through one ray of this Love all other love exists.

7   The fourth is the love of man for man. The love which exists between the hearts of believers is prompted by the ideal of the unity of spirits. This love is attained through the knowledge of God, so that men see the Divine Love reflected in the heart. Each sees in the other the Beauty of God reflected in the soul, and finding this point of similarity, they are attracted to one another in love. This love will make all men the waves of one sea, this love will make them all the stars of one heaven and the fruits of one tree. This love will bring the realization of true accord, the foundation of real unity.

8   But the love which sometimes exists between friends is not (true) love, because it is subject to transmutation; this is merely fascination. As the breeze blows, the slender trees yield. If the wind is in the East the tree leans to the West, and if the wind turns to the West the tree leans to the East. This kind of love is originated by the accidental conditions of life. This is not love, it is merely acquaintanceship; it is subject to change.

9   Today you will see two souls apparently in close friendship; tomorrow all this may be changed. Yesterday they were

ready to die for one another, today they shun one another's society! This is not love; it is the yielding of the hearts to the accidents of life. When that which has caused this "love" to exist passes, the love passes also; this is not in reality love.

Love is only of the four kinds that I have explained. (a) 10 The love of God towards the identity of God. Christ has said God is Love. (b) The love of God for His children—for His servants. (c) The love of man for God and (d) the love of man for man. These four kinds of love originate from God. These are rays from the Sun of Reality; these are the Breathings of the Holy Spirit; these are the Signs of the Reality.

59

TABLET REVEALED
BY 'ABDU'L-BAHÁ

August 28th, 1913

O Thou my beloved daughter! 1

Thine eloquent and fluent letter was perused in a garden, 2
under the cool shade of a tree, while the gentle breeze was
wafting. The means of physical enjoyment was spread before
the eyes and thy letter became the cause of spiritual enjoyment. Truly, I say, it was not a letter but a rose-garden adorned
with hyacinths and flowers.

It contained the sweet fragrance of paradise and the zephyr 3
of Divine Love blew from its roseate words.

As I have not ample time at my disposal, I will give herein 4
a brief, conclusive and comprehensive answer. It is as follows:

In this Revelation of Bahá'u'lláh, the women go neck and 5
neck with the men. In no movement will they be left behind.
Their rights with men are equal in degree. They will enter all
the administrative branches of politics. They will attain in all
such a degree as will be considered the very highest station of
the world of humanity and will take part in all affairs. Rest
ye assured. Do ye not look upon the present conditions; in

the not far distant future the world of women will become all-refulgent and all-glorious, *For His Holiness Bahá'u'lláh Hath Willed It so!* At the time of elections the right to vote is the inalienable right of women, and the entrance of women into all human departments is an irrefutable and incontrovertible question. No soul can retard or prevent it.

6   But there are certain matters, the participation in which is not worthy of women. For example, at the time when the community is taking up vigorous defensive measures against the attack of foes, the women are exempt from military engagements. It may so happen that at a given time warlike and savage tribes may furiously attack the body politic with the intention of carrying on a wholesale slaughter of its members; under such a circumstance defense is necessary, but it is the duty of men to organize and execute such defensive measures and not the women—because their hearts are tender and they cannot endure the sight of the horror of carnage, even if it is for the sake of defense. From such and similar undertakings the women are exempt.

7   As regards the constitution of the House of Justice, Bahá'u'lláh addresses the men. He says: "O ye men of the House of Justice!"

8   But when its members are to be elected, the right which belongs to women, so far as their voting and their voice is concerned, is indisputable. When the women attain to the ultimate degree of progress, then, according to the exigency of the time and place and their great capacity, they shall obtain extraordinary privileges. Be ye confident on these accounts. His Holiness Bahá'u'lláh has greatly strengthened the cause of women, and the rights and privileges of women is one of the greatest principles of 'Abdu'l-Bahá. Rest ye assured!

Erelong the days shall come when the men addressing the women, shall say: *"Blessed are ye! Blessed are ye! Verily ye are worthy of every gift. Verily ye deserve to adorn your heads with the crown of everlasting glory, because in sciences and arts, in virtues and perfections ye shall become equal to man, and as regards tenderness of heart and the abundance of mercy and sympathy ye are superior."*

Index

References to the words of 'Abdu'l-Bahá are indexed by talk number, followed by paragraph number.

For more information about the Bahá'í Faith,
or to contact the Bahá'ís near you, visit
http://www.bahai.us/
or call
1-800-22-UNITE

PUBLISHING

BAHÁ'Í PUBLISHING
AND THE BAHÁ'Í FAITH

Bahá'í Publishing produces books based on the teachings of the Bahá'í Faith. Founded over 160 years ago, the Bahá'í Faith has spread to some 235 nations and territories and is now accepted by more than five million people. The word "Bahá'í" means "follower of Bahá'u'lláh." Bahá'u'lláh, the founder of the Bahá'í Faith, asserted that He is the Messenger of God for all of humanity in this day. The cornerstone of His teachings is the establishment of the spiritual unity of humankind, which will be achieved by personal transformation and the application of clearly identified spiritual principles. Bahá'ís also believe that there is but one religion and that all the Messengers of God—among them Abraham, Zoroaster, Moses, Krishna, Buddha, Jesus, and Muḥammad—have progressively revealed its nature. Together, the world's great religions are expressions of a single, unfolding divine plan. Human beings, not God's Messengers, are the source of religious divisions, prejudices, and hatreds.

The Bahá'í Faith is not a sect or denomination of another religion, nor is it a cult or a social movement. Rather, it is a globally recognized independent world religion founded on new books of scripture revealed by Bahá'u'lláh.

Bahá'í Publishing is an imprint of the National Spiritual Assembly of the Bahá'ís of the United States.

For more information about the Bahá'í Faith,
or to contact Bahá'ís near you,
visit http://www.bahai.us/
or call
1-800-22-UNITE